QUICK GUIDE TO
INSIGHT
SALES

I0076249

QUICK GUIDE TO
INSIGHT
SALES

GET SMARTER.
GET THE S.P.I.C.E³

GARY R. FORD MBA, PHD
IN CONSULTATION WITH BERNIE SPAK

Quick Guide To
Insight Sales
Get SMARTER. Get The S.P.I.C.E³

Published by Insight Publishers
Address: Thorsby, Alberta, Canada
Website: http//garyrford.ca/insight
Edited, designed and typeset by the Author
Printed in the United States of America or Canada
ISBN: 978-0-9939737-8-9

Copyright © 2016 by Gary R. Ford

All rights reserved. No portion of this publication may be reproduced, stored in a retrieval system, or transmitted in any form or by any means – electronic, mechanical, photocopy, recording, scanning, or other – except in the case of brief quotations embodied in critical reviews or articles, without the prior written permission of the publisher.

Limit of Liability/Disclaimer of Warranty

The publisher and author disclaim any implied warranties and make no guarantees whatsoever that you will achieve any particular result in your own use of the materials contained herein. The publisher and author shall not be held liable for any loss of profit, income or any other commercial damages, including but not limited to special, incidental, consequential or other damages. The fact that a book, author, organization, or website is referred to in this work as a citation and/or potential source of information does not mean that the publisher or author endorses the information such resources might provide. The examples presented here in were fabricated for instructional purposes and for variety to show behaviour in different sales environments.

DEDICATION

Dedicated to all salespeople who previously read one of our Insight Sales books and saw enough of interest that they want to further develop their selling skills so that both they and their customers achieve greater success.

Table Of Contents

INTRODUCTION

This Quick Guide to Insight Sales is intended as a companion to any one of the three other Insight Sales books:

1. Insight Sales (Retail) – specifically for the retail salesperson.

2. Insight Sales (Corporate) – specifically for the corporate or outbound salesperson.

3. Insight Sales (Corporate and Retail) – specifically for the salesperson that works in a hybrid role of sometimes engaging incoming customers in a show room or retail setting and sometimes journeying out to meet clients in their own environments.

Think of this book as the student's notes version of one of these three books – those bits and pieces that a serious reader might have hi-lighted with a yellow marker as he read any one of the Insight Sales books.

The Quick Guide describes the sturdy bones of Insight Sales. However, as content was stripped out of the larger versions, the flesh and muscle of what makes up Insight Selling was also stripped away. The Quick Guide presents substantially less of the rational, underlying values, and examples for all that is the Insight Sales approach. For that, you need to read one of the full books on Insight Sales. The Quick Guide gives you the mechanics of Insight Sales as a quick reference to remind you what to do as you work to implement this approach in your own work.

I recommend that you obtain the full Insight Sales book that best fits your sales situation and learn more about the rationale for Insight Sales. You will find more examples, deeper explanations for why the salesperson does what he or she does in this approach, and more about the underlying values that shape the salesperson's behavior when he or she is committed to effective Insight Sales. Then, use this Quick Guide as a reference, a reminder of the sequence to follow, and what to do at each step, as you help your clients to achieve new insights and greater success.

READINESS TO BUY

In order to get ready to buy, an individual has to move from the comfort of his or her status quo, recognize that he or she has problems and needs, and anticipate how better results can be achieved with an appropriate solution. Selling is all about helping your customer move into that readiness to buy, then providing the right solution to the customer's needs.

Because of a natural tendency to deny problems and their costs, the salesperson must help the customer to move from,

"Things are okay the way they are." (*current situation*)

to

"Well, we're frustrated by… but I can live with it." (*problems*)

through

"I guess the costs are bigger than I thought." (*implications*)

and

"I can't do anything because…." (*constraints*)

to

"You mean there are other possibilities? (*minimal expectations*)

shifting to

"Wow! The benefits would be….". (*exciting benefits*)

and finally to

"How do I do this?" (*eagerness*)

The customer is more motivated to buy when he or she achieves greater clarity about:

- his or her current situation,
- the problem(s) he or she has in the current situation,
- the implications of those problems – what the problems cost the customer, how much frustration he or she has, and what is the pain of the status quo,

2

- the real <u>constraints</u> or reasons keeping him or her from doing something about this before now, and

- his or her minimal <u>expectations</u> about what a solution would have to accomplish, his or her <u>excitements</u> about the extra benefits to be gained by effectively solving the problem(s), and his or her <u>eagerness</u> to get the problem(s) solved.

This process involves exploring the reality of the customer's situation and experiencing the emotions that go along with consideration of the costs of the customer's problems and the impediments to achieving better results. People are more willing and enthusiastic about making buying decisions when helped to mentally organize what they discover about their own S.P.I.C.E^3. It is the salesperson's job to help people to examine their own status quo and arrive at a readiness for a new solution.

The S.P.I.C.E^3

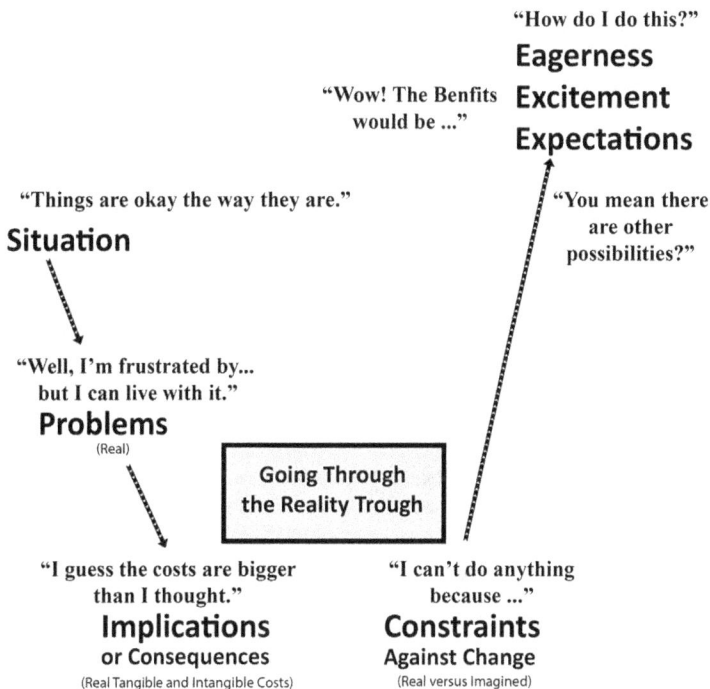

To be effective, you need to be able to get into a S.P.I.C.E[3] conversation with each customer. When you do, you will be selling to customers eager to buy the solutions you sell. You must be the catalyst that shifts each customer to a readiness to buy.

THE REALITY TROUGH

You must take the customer into and through his or her Reality Trough.

Salesperson's Responsibility
Shift The Disinterested, Resistant and Low Motivation Customer

Be willing to let emotions emerge as the customer considers the costs of his or her problems and the constraints that prevent action. These feelings need to rise to the surface of the customer's awareness. Through this insight, the customer will be more aware of his or her need to solve the problem(s) and be much more motivated to buy an effective solution. This process of helping the customer to better understand his S.P.I.C.E[3], is called Insight Selling.

Understand this process. See it as your responsibility to take your customers through this S.P.I.C.E[3] cycle, bring about new insights, and help your customers to get ready for change. Then find the proper solutions for their needs.

GET SMARTER

Use a sales approach that best fits with how and why customers become inspired to buy new solutions. Insight Selling has two halves. The first half is about getting information from the customer the salesperson needs to know in order to recommend a complete solution that satisfies the customer's needs. The second half is about helping the customer to achieve greater success by providing that solution.

Use a sales approach that best fits with how and why customers become inspired to buy new solutions. In this modern economy, the most effective sales process is both consultative and insight-oriented in nature. The focus is on a deeper discovery of the customer's real and full set of needs. The salesperson helps the customer to achieve deeper insights about the nature of how he or she falls short of what could be achieved.

The salesperson's conversations reframe the customer's understanding of his or her own situation, problems, costs, constraints and opportunities. Before any product, service or solution is offered, the salesperson creates value by delivering new insights. Because of this new understanding, these customers set higher goals, make larger purchases, and achieve greater success.

Once insight has been achieved as to the real problem(s) to be solved and the reasons why, the sales person engages in problem solving on the customer's behalf to come up with the right solution to the customer's needs. The salesperson considers his or her role as one of helping clients to achieve greater success, and urges the customer to take action to solve problems and experience benefits as soon as possible.

The interaction between salesperson and customer is so different from traditional methods of selling because it involves working with customers instead of doing something to them. The insight approach is usually more profitable for all parties. This approach is used with the goal of achieving sales that are profitable both for the client, the selling organization, and the salesperson.

The sales process involves two-way communication emphasizing both information giving and open negotiation, but the customer will be encouraged to do about 70% of the talking. Customers open up and share a lot more information about themselves, their problems and their expectations. More rapport is established and the customer feels more comfortable with the salesperson. The customer's story is usually much larger and as a result, sales are usually larger. These sales typically involve complex solutions for complex problems.

Specifically, smart salespeople use an approach – the ten step "GET SMARTER" insight-oriented approach – that includes processes to learn the customer's S.P.I.C.E^3 and specific skills proven to increase sales effectiveness.

G	Greet	A greeting and approach by the salesperson showing interest in the customer and beginning a conversation.
E	Engage	Continued engagement in conversation, allowing relationship building to occur.
T	Take Time To Learn Customer's Needs – Get the S.P.I.C.E^3	Getting the customer's S.P.I.C.E^3 during an open discussion of the customer's needs, by actively listening to the customer such that the customer does most of the talking while the salesperson clarifies for understanding (*reaching for deeper insight*).
	Half Time	*Determining the best possible solution, preparing to make the recommendation and if necessary, rehearsing how to show full understanding before a recommendation is made.*
S	Show Full Understanding – Summarize The Customer's S.P.I.C.E^3	Before trying to sell anything, showing full understanding by summarizing what has been learned about the customer's needs and expectations, and then asking if you fully understand. Summarizing in the order of the customer's S.P.I.C.E^3, stirring up the feelings of the customer's Reality Trough, so the customer arrives at eagerness to hear/see the solution.
M	Make Your Recommendation	Recommending the complete solution by referring to the benefits the customer is hoping to achieve.
A	Ask How To Proceed	Asking for a decision and initiating a call-to-action by simply asking the customer what he or she thinks should happen next.
R	Reinforce The Customer's Decision	Reinforcing the benefits of the customer's decision and letting the customer know he or she has made a wise choice.

T	Thank You and Follow-Up (After Sale Support and Service)	Thanking the customer for the opportunity to earn his or her business, helping the customer through the purchase transaction, and staying in contact with the customer as part of the on-going relationship.
E	Evaluate	Assessing your performance in three ways - through measurement of the results clients have realized with the solutions you provided, customer feedback, and self-analysis.
R	Repeat	Returning to the beginning and repeating the insight-oriented selling process with both new and existing clients.

Use this ten step model as an agenda you take into each meeting you have with a customer. With this roadmap in mind, you will have more comfort during your conversations with all kinds of customer types.

THE FIRST HALF OF THE SELLING PROCESS

> *Your first task isn't to pitch your product, or to sell something, but to get to know the real needs of your potential client. Get The customer's S.P.I.C.E[3]. Half of your selling time should be spent on this first half. This is a radical shift from traditional selling.*

STEP ONE – GREET YOUR CUSTOMERS

You can't sell without getting into meaningful conversations with potential buyers – and lots of them. Begin that conversation with your greeting.

To be successful using the "GET SMARTER" approach, create a relationship with your customer by engaging him or her in an open conversation.

THE GOALS OF THE GREETING STEP

- Gain an opportunity to talk face-to-face with potential customers.

- Create a positive first impression for you and your organization.

- Help the customer to feel comfortable and valued, and if you are in a retail environment, welcome in your store.

- Introduce yourself so the customer knows enough about you to feel comfortable having you in his or her space; or if you are in a retail location, make your presence known to each customer that comes into your store or store section.

- Establish your credibility as someone that can help.

- Begin a conversation where you can learn about the customer.

and

- Get as many customers as you can to accept that conversation with you.

With this greeting, begin a larger conversation where you and the customer can find out what the real problems are, and then help the customer to find a complete solution to those problems.

IMPORTANT ELEMENTS OF GREETING

Performance of an effective greeting is critical to success with every customer. The way you greet will significantly determine whether or not you even have a chance to sell. In the first few moments of your encounter, clearly show each customer you are someone who has value to offer. Be seen as someone who can be trusted. Show that you are there to look after the customer's needs. Get each customer to talk with you.

ENSURE A POSITIVE FIRST IMPRESSION

Create a positive first impression which will be influenced by many things, some of which are:

- how you dress and your personal grooming,

- your activities at the time you first encounter the customer,

- your underlying attitudes,

- your demeanour and how you carry yourself (*which is heavily influenced by your attitudes*),

- the expectations you have about the customer's possible reaction, and

- your initial greeting behaviour (*what you say and what you do*).

You want this first impression to make the customer receptive to your approach.

Bernie Spak, a professional salesperson, says, "Building rapport and trust with a customer through a positive first impression takes a conscious effort. This is an important part of building your personal brand as a salesperson. Ultimately what the customer experiences with you in the sales process will define your brand, but that initial impression is like a well thought out logo or book cover."

DRESS AND GROOMING

The general guideline here is that the salesperson should dress as expected by his or her typical customers. You need to dress to impress the typical customers that you encounter in your sales role.

Outbound salespeople are generally expected to be in business attire. Typically this involves a business suit, clean shirt, and dress shoes, whether one is male or female. For males, a tie is typically expected.

In the retail environment, dress is more typically casual business attire, including dress slacks and a clean shirt, often of the golf shirt variety. In some large chains, there may be a retail uniform. Be at your designated position "dressed for business".

Consider your personal appearance, your hygiene, your tone of voice, and your body language. Is it appealing enough, fresh enough, eager enough, and relevant enough in the environment you sell in to get people engaged? Or does it turn people away and create immediate resistance that will take additional time to overcome?

ACTIVITIES WHEN ENCOUNTERING CUSTOMERS

In outbound sales, you can use certain activities to establish your presence and role in the client's environment. Enter, shake hands and when the invitation to sit comes from the customer, do so quickly and get a pen and portfolio ready so you can take notes.

In the retail environment, customers are generally wary when they enter a store. However customers are seldom wary when they see a person who is busy and working hard. They aren't threatened when they see someone carrying stock to the retail floor, arranging product so it is more accessible on the shelves, placing new outfits on mannequins, improving product demonstrations, cleaning or dusting. Do helpful housekeeping work on the retail floor. If busy merchandising when the customer approaches you, greet the customer effectively to show him or her that your retail establishment is a good place to be and let the customer tell you why he or she approached you.

UNDERLYING ATTITUDES AND YOUR PERSONAL DEMEANOUR

Think of every customer as someone who will buy, but first get to know the customer's needs and interests. Hold the attitude this person is worth knowing, and prepare to add to this customer's well being.

Your own success depends on helping each customer to succeed, to achieve more. Do this by establishing rapport and winning trust. Approach in order to get to know, not to get a sale.

Hold a personal demeanour of confidence, mixed with humility and compassion for your fellow beings. Do not come across as arrogant. Do not come across as being motivated to just get a sale. Approach with the goal of getting to know this customer and his or her needs.

Your demeanour comes from your beliefs and attitudes, your goals and motivations. To be effective using the Insight Sales approach, hold beliefs, attitudes, goals and motivations that favour the customer's success.

YOUR EXPECTATIONS

The expectations you have about the customer's possible reaction to your approach will also show. Approach without any expectation as to how the customer will react to your greeting. Have an open mind, assume anything is possible, and give the customer the chance to react in his or her own way. Watch, listen, and feel the customer's reaction, then meet the customer in his or her moment.

YOUR INITIAL GREETING BEHAVIOUR

What you say and what you do can make a difference. Greet your customer with:

- a warm and sincere smile,

- good eye contact, especially when he or she talks to you,

- a non-threatening position relative to the customer's personal space,

- an erect and open body posture, or when sitting, being upright, with a portfolio resting in your lap, hands on the portfolio, and legs closed,

- a sincere, enthusiastic, and appreciative attitude, plus

- a warm, humble, attentive expression of interest in working with the customer.

Be clean, free of unpleasant odours, well groomed, and wearing clean presentable clothing.

People have a personal space and a salesperson needs to be sensitive to what that spatial zone is for each customer. Be close enough but not too close, usually just under three feet of distance – an arms length.

(If you only work in retail sales, you might want to jump to page 22)

CORPORATE OR OUTBOUND SALES

In the corporate sales environment, you must find ways to wind up sitting in front of the person with the problems your products and services can solve. Engage in information gathering activities before you even approach a potential customer.

IDENTIFY YOUR SOLUTIONS

Take a look at what you sell. Figure out how the products and services can work together to solve problems for potential customers. Get out of the product and commodity focus and think about solving problems.

IDENTIFY THE PROBLEMS YOUR SOLUTIONS SOLVE

Once you have identified how your products and services can be mixed together as solutions, identify the problems that would predictably benefit from the solutions you and your company sell. Learn as much as you can about those problems and how your company's products and services are suitable solutions.

Identify the typical symptoms that reveal the existence of these problems, both the obvious symptoms and those that might not be so obvious to potential customers. Look for the most critical symptoms that have the greatest costs.

What do these problems typically cost? What are the financial, emotional, and lost opportunity consequences of such problems? Build a good understanding of problem implications. Then learn the typical consequences that matter to each type of customer or to each level within an organization.

LEARN ABOUT DIFFERENT BUSINESS MANAGER FUNCTIONAL RESPONSIBILITIES

Do these problems show up in production, marketing, sales, research and development, inventory and supply management, human resources management, financing, logistics or other corporate functions? Who are the people within target organizations that are accountable for these problems and who is impacted? Learn as much as you can about these different business functions so you can speak the functional business languages of the responsible managers.

LEARN ABOUT POTENTIAL CUSTOMERS

Then identify companies or individual consumers that would predictably benefit from the solutions, products and services you and your company sell.

Your employer probably has some idea about potential companies or individuals that are not yet customers. Learn as much as you can about each of them. Look at a list of who is buying from your company and then look for other similar companies or persons that are not yet customers. If you sell to businesses, consider the competitors of your existing customers. Consider whole industry groups that your company hasn't yet sold to. If you sell to individuals, consider professions that you haven't yet approached or common interest groups that include pools of potential customers for your solutions.

Gathering Individual Information

Your research can involve use of the Internet to gather information about target customers. Find people that might benefit from your solutions in Facebook or Linked-In and learn all you can about them. Engage people socially and learn about them. Be the person that approaches strangers, opens up a conversation and actively listens to discover who the person is, what he or she does, his or her interests, his or her goals and desires, any problems that impede achievement of greater success. Listen first. Talk second.

Gathering Corporate Intelligence

Again, you can use the Internet to gather corporate intelligence. Corporations use their websites to tell you a lot about their business. Customers share reviews. The news media posts on-line stories about industries and industry participants.

In addition, the business section of your local newspaper may have done a profile on a target business. Trade journals may do stories on particular companies within the industry they cover. Libraries keep copies of such papers and can be a helpful resource.

Talk to customers of potential target companies. Identify some of the target company's suppliers. Investigate the type of hiring the target company does, as companies hire people to solve business problems. Examine how they get their products to the market place? Study what they say about themselves in their advertising and public promotions? If a public company, look for the information they make available to investors. Find ways to meet with specific employees of the target company.

Social networking sites can give you information about potential clients. Search for people who work for the organizations that are of interest to you and obtain information they might post. These sites typically allow you to contact the people you are following, and this might allow conversations where you can obtain important information.

As you do this research, build a folder or computer file of information for each potential customer you identify.

PREPARATION

Develop a concise package of information about yourself and your company that you will later send to or leave with your customers. This package should clearly indicate that you sell solutions (*not just products*) related to problems likely experienced by your target customers. You want this package to be easily read, brief, and likely to be opened.

In this package, provide one element of insight for the target customer, perhaps making the customer aware of the significance of certain symptoms. Include testimonials presenting examples of how you and your company have worked with other organizations or other individuals like them. Prepare a sheet including an example of cost savings, revenue increases and profit gains a customer could expect, along with any intangible gains they might attain.

Be strategic about when you give this packet to your customers. You could include it in a first mailing to a potential client to introduce yourself, or you could leave it with a customer after your first meeting.

SEND A LETTER OF INTRODUCTION

If you are selling to a corporation, you will ideally send this letter to the most significant person that resides within your sales territory. Aim for the top. If this is the president of the company, send a letter to him or her. Know about the target company and the person you are contacting so you can make your letter particularly significant to him or her.

Similarly, if you sell to individuals, know as much as you can and make reference to what you know. This letter should clearly be a personalized letter to the individual and not a commonly used form letter. Keep these letters down to a very readable one page in length.

- State who you are and the company you work for, and indicate the benefits of meeting with you.

- Indicate your desire to arrange an appointment to meet with the recipient to discuss how your company might be able to help him or her with a specific problem or set of problems.

- State the solution areas in which you and your company have established your expertise.

- List some of the symptoms that might make such a meeting relevant to the recipient.

- Describe how you are differentiated from your competition.

- List examples of how your company has helped other customers increase their success.

- Indicate when you would be available to get together and give several options.

- Advise the recipient you will call to schedule such a meeting.

- Include your telephone contact information in the signature portion of the letter.

If you have one available, include an informative article relating to the problems that parallel, or could parallel problems the potential client might be experiencing. In a hand written note on the article, indicate that your company and your partner company, if one is involved, have expertise in these areas.

CALL THE CUSTOMER

After the customer has had time to receive your introductory letter, call when you indicated you would. Remind him or her who you are and that you are calling as promised in your letter. Ask if he or she has time to take a short call now. If not, ask when would be a better time to call.

If this person does have time for your call, explain who you are and indicate that your job is helping similar people to achieve greater success. Indicate you've helped customers with particular problems (*list them*) and ask if you could have thirty minutes of his or her time in a face-to-face meeting to discuss how this might be relevant to the customer's own situation.

> "Sarah, thank you for taking my call. I'm asking for five minutes of your time right now to determine if my company might be able to work with your company. Is this convenient?"

If the person you call states he or she does not believe your solutions fit his or her needs, but you have some intelligence indicating the customer may in fact have related problems, then you could ask very pertinent S.P.I.C.E^3 questions in this call. Later in this book, we'll present many examples of S.P.I.C.E^3 questions. These questions would be selected based on what you think you've already learned.

Alternatively, you could tell this person about your research methods and offer to meet to share what you learned about the customer and how you learned this information from his or her customers, employees, suppliers and competitors. You want to stimulate the other person's curiosity and impress him or her with the preparation work you have done.

PRESENT AT SPECIAL INTEREST GROUP MEETINGS

Arrange to make presentations at Special Interest Group meetings on a topic you are comfortable speaking about. Such special interest group or speaking opportunities could include:

- President's Clubs
- Professional Associations
- Industry Associations
- Serious Hobby Clubs
- Community College Extension courses
- Courses at industry events

- Chamber of Commerce mixers

This shouldn't be a sales pitch session, but an informative session about solutions to problems the attendees might experience. Deliver insights to build your credibility.

Gain a relationship with each participant. Develop trust. This is not an opportunity for you to do a sales pitch. Use the skills for effective listening and create an open discussion.

OFFER PROBLEM SPECIFIC SEMINARS

One way to find individuals or businesses that might have problems addressed by your solutions is to offer problem specific seminars. Promote yourself as an expert speaker on such problems and offer seminars that describe the issues and share the solutions you have seen applied. Give anecdotal information about the successes your previous clients achieved.

BE A GUEST ON VARIOUS MEDIA

In some markets, you might be able to offer your services as an expert guest on talk radio or morning television programs. Give very specific and practical advice. Be seen as someone who is helpful, knows what he or she is talking about, and is an available expert for those with problems you can solve.

IF ALL ELSE FAILS – USE THE PRODUCT APPROACH

If such non-product approaches fail to work, then resort to a product-oriented approach. Identify the products and services your company can offer at very competitive prices. Then contact possible customers – likely someone in the corporate Purchasing department. Call and ask for an opportunity to present your products and services. Indicate some compelling reason for this person to want to talk with you.

Once face-to-face, hold back on your product pitch and listen using the S.P.I.C.E^3 questions and active listening skills presented later in this book. Get the customer talking. The customer may ask about the product you called him or her about. If so, answer the questions and use the skills to open up a broader conversation. Lead the conversation to an exploration of the customer's S.P.I.C.E.[3]

THE CORPORATE OR OUTBOUND SALES GREETING

- Once you've obtained your appointment, prepare yourself in advance by reviewing your research notes about this potential client.

- Remember, you've been invited into someone else's space. Be grateful for that invitation, and show respect.

- Arrive on time.

- When face-to-face, approach the customer offering a firm but not over-powering handshake, make eye contact, state your name and thank him or her for this opportunity to meet.

- Be comfortable, confident that you have value to add, and be respectful of the person you meet.

- Let the customer respond however he or she does, while watching closely for any clues about his or her emotional state.

- Check to see if this is still an acceptable time to meet. Offer to re-schedule and meet at a later time if the person needs to postpone.

- If the customer looks comfortable meeting with you, then proceed.

- Explain how you work as a salesperson. Explain your goal of learning the needs of your client and working with him or her to help the customer achieve greater success.

- If the customer doesn't appear ready to tell you about him or herself, give an example or two of things you've done with other clients and the achieved results.

This is not the time to pitch your products or services. Instead, offer to work with the client to discuss his or her needs and to determine if you can help by finding solutions with better results.

"Hello Mr. Fitzgerald. I appreciate your agreeing to meet with me. My name is (*your name*) and I represent (*name of your company*). I know your time is precious and respect what you have allotted for this conversation. I called because my company has helped companies like X, Y, and Z (*companies similar to this customer's company*) to improve their (*what the customer does*) resulting in reduced costs and increased revenues. I would like to explore the potential of doing this with your company. To do so, I'd like to learn more about how your company does..."

(If you only work in corporate or outbound sales, you might want to skip ahead to page 27)

THE RETAIL GREETING AND APPROACH

People appear in your store and you have the opportunity to approach them to provide assistance. If someone is shopping in your store, it's safe to assume there is a problem to solve. Your task is to find out what the problem is, and then sell a complete solution.

- welcome the customer to your place of business,

- help the customer to feel comfortable talking with you, and

- set the stage for a conversation during which you and the customer can discover the customer's S.P.I.C.E[3].

GREETING VERSUS APPROACH

A greeting typically occurs when you speak to the customer as he or she walks past you, or approaches you. In the greeting, you welcome the customer and offer to provide directions. Stand ninety degrees to the side of the walkway and speak as the customer passes by.

"Good morning, welcome to (*the name of your store*). May I direct you to what you're looking for?"

The customer may say, "Thanks but I'm just looking." If so, turn the customer's reaction to your greeting into a conversation by saying something like,

"Great. We have a lot of stuff to browse. If you tell me what you're looking for, I'll be glad to show you where it's located."

If the customer insists he or she is okay without help, say something like,

"Enjoy your visit. Likely, one of us will check in with you periodically to see if you have any questions."

As this is a greeting, and not an approach, you're **not yet** moving toward the customer. When any customer passes you by, offer a greeting.

An approach is what you do when you go toward a customer. Be sensitive to the timing of your approach. Watch the customer's behaviour and see when he or she is ready. Give the person time to come in, orient him or herself, and settle down. Typically the customer would be at least 30 feet inside your store, or in the middle of the store if you work in a smaller location, before you approach.

If you see the customer looking about as if looking for a salesperson, or standing and looking at specific products, it's probably safe to approach. There are different ways to approach and greet your customers.

THE "WELCOME" APPROACH

This approach involves a specific statement of welcome. You walk up to the customer, welcome the person to the store, and get him or her to talk with you. Approach, stop just over an arm's length away, and say,

"Welcome to (_the name of your store_)! My name is (_your first name_), and how may I be of assistance?

THE MERCHANDISE APPROACH

Speak to the customer when he or she is looking at specific items of merchandise. Walk up, stand to the customer's side just over an arm's length away, and say something like,

"Looks like you're in the market for a new XXXXXXX today? (_pause_)"

Refer to the type of product the customer is looking at. This should be offered as a question inviting the customer to speak to you about what he or she is shopping for. Get customers telling you about the interests in the products they have in their hands or they're looking at on the shelves.

THE "I HAVE SOMETHING FOR YOU" APPROACH

Offer the customer a gift to start the relationship off. Approach the customer, give something of value, and get into a conversation. You could say something like,

"Our flyer this week offers some really compelling savings that might interest you. Here's a copy for you to examine. Was there anything in particular you were shopping for today?"

THE FRIEDMAN 180° PASS-BY NON-BUSINESS APPROACH

Harry Friedman, an expert on retail selling, teaches the "180 degree pass-by" method. Actually walk as if you're just passing by, get past the customer, turn, and ask a question, preferably something personal about the customer. You might pass, turn and say,

"I just noticed the lapel pin for (*name of a local charitable organization*). I'm a supporter. What's your involvement with them?"

THE FRIENDLY NEIGHBOUR APPROACH

As a friendly, non-business approach simply say,

"Hi. How are you doing today?"

Or notice something unique about the person, and use this to start a conversation.

"I see you're wearing a blood donors badge. My brother was just in an accident and needed blood, so thank you for your contribution. Is this something you do regularly?"

The "How's The Weather?" Approach

Ask "How's the weather?" but attempt to be different in how you do so by saying something more specific to the customer.

"Great tan. I'm guessing it's quite sunny out today?"

or

"Wow, you're clothes are quite wet. It must be raining heavily out there?"

The "Can I Help You?" Approach

Although most sales teachers say don't use the "Can I help You?" approach, you can deliberately use it to turn the customer's reflexive brush off response ("I'm just browsing.") into humour.

"That's great. Browsing can be fun... but it can be dangerous too. You might be seduced by some impulse to buy. Be careful out there."

Use humour, and playfulness. Get the customer smiling, chuckling or laughing with you, and continue the conversation.

Dealing With the Brush Off

If you do get a "brush off" response from a customer, use an effective comeback to remain engaged.

"That's great, we want you to enjoy your visit to (*the name of your store*). However, we don't want to ignore you. So if you need any assistance, please don't hesitate to ask either myself or one of my colleagues."

As you say this, make good eye contact and watch for the customer to immediately ask you for help.

Non-verbal "Go Away" Clues

The customer may give you non-verbal clues showing he or she wants to be left alone, or wants to distance him or herself from you:

- a step back,

- a look away,

- brief and briefer answers to your queries, or

- focusing his or her attention on product and trying to ignore you.

If the customer does this, say something like,

> "It seems you want some space to shop on your own for a few minutes. That's okay. We want you to enjoy your visit to (_the name of your store_). However, we don't want to ignore you. If you need any assistance, please don't hesitate to ask either myself or one of my colleagues."

Stay alert and watch for new clues the customer wants assistance.

> *Unfortunately, you also need to be watchful that the customer didn't insist on being left alone to shoplift .*

WHEN TO MOVE TO ENGAGING

You know it's time to transition when:

- the customer smiles at you,

- he or she maintains eye contact with you,

- you feel like you've initiated some small degree of rapport with the customer,

- the customer makes a conversational reply,

- the customer begins to share information about his or her needs,

- the customer starts talking about your products, or

- the customer tells you what he or she is looking for.

It should take only a few seconds, from the point at which you initiate your Greeting to the transition to Step Two where you more fully engage in conversation.

THE TRANSITION WHEN IN RETAIL

There are several ways to transition to the next step when in a retail environment :

1. Engage in whatever social chitchat the customer offers up.

   "Yes, the Oilers were very impressive last night. I really enjoyed that game. I watched on TV. Did you go to the game itself?"

2. Share something of yourself that might be of interest to the customer.

   "That's a great XXXXXX. I use that myself."

3. Paraphrase whatever response he or she gives to your greeting.

   "Sounds like you've come to get some _____ supplies?"

4. Answer any questions the customer asks. Be helpful and positively responsive. Be enthusiastic.

   "Yes that XXXXXX will do a wonderful job at ____."

or

5. Ask your own transitional question to move the focus on to what the customer is shopping for.

   "So what's the special occasion that brings you in today?"

You want to meet the customer in his or her moment, socializing if that is what he or she offers; or use a transitional question to remind the customer he or she had a purpose, something that motivated him or her to come out shopping.

THE TRANSITION WHEN IN CORPORATE OR OUTBOUND SALES

In a corporate or outbound sales meeting, you have the same options:

1. engage in whatever social chitchat the customer offers up,

2. share something of yourself that might be of interest to the customer,

3. paraphrase whatever response he or she gives to your greeting,

4. answer any questions the customer asks you, being helpful, positively responsive, and enthusiastic, or

5. ask your own transitional question to move the focus on to the customer's interests that caused him or her to meet with you.

Steer the conversation toward the customer telling you about his or her situation and any business problems related to your products and services.

> "I'd like to see if our company could be equally helpful to your company. Please tell me more about how you do what you do and if you experience (*list the symptoms of the problems your solutions solve*)?"

STEP TWO – ENGAGING

> *It's not enough to simply introduce yourself and your company to the customer. Cause an open conversation to occur and a working relationship to begin. Build rapport, credibility, and show the customer you have value.*

Engaging will allow you to transition from the greeting to learning about the customer's needs.

THE GOALS OF THE ENGAGING STEP

- Get the customer into a conversation with you, most typically by talking about what is of interest to the customer.

- Build rapport with this customer so he or she is comfortable talking with you.

and

- Set the stage to begin a focus on the customer's needs.

First, "meet the customer in his or her moment" and then steer the interaction to a conversation about his or her needs. The goal is to enter a conversation where you're able to learn the customer's S.P.I.C.E^3.

IN THE RETAIL ENVIRONMENT

Some customers want to talk with a salesperson, explain their interests and get advice, while many others seem to want to be left alone to shop on their own. However, most customers would be better off receiving the help of an ethical and knowledgeable insight-oriented consultant who discovers their needs, deepens the customer's insight and recommends the right solution to those needs. Engage all your retail customers in a conversation that opens up the customer's S.P.I.C.E^3.

IN THE CORPORATE SALES ENVIRONMENT

Similarly, corporate customers typically haven't encountered salespeople who are insight-oriented consultants helping them to solve business problems. If the salesperson calmly greets and then engages the customer in a conversation based on what is presented in the customer's moment, then listens and attends to what is on the customer's mind, the customer retains control of the conversation. The customer will feel more comfortable. You work to manage the conversation toward an opening for exploration of the customer's needs.

ENGAGING EFFECTIVELY

Get people talking with you, even when at first they don't want to do so. Establish trust and rapport early in the conversation, so the customer will open up to you. Meet the customer in his or her moment and use what is relevant to the customer to get your conversation going. Don't treat all customers the same way. Pay attention to how he or she acts when you greet the customer and adjust your behaviour accordingly.

If the customer has questions, answer the questions, then ask a question of your own. If he or she wants to negotiate about price, engage the customer in negotiation without giving anything away, and then ask what he or she will be using the discussed solution for. Engage in a few moments of chitchat if that is initiated by the customer, or if you need to do so to feel more comfortable in the conversation. Start from what appears to be important to the customer and then steer the conversation to a more open discussion of his or her needs.

ENGAGEMENT STRATEGIES

GET PAST THE FOCUS ON PRODUCT

Your customer may ask you about a product or specific service. First paraphrase the question to make sure you understand what the customer is really asking. Once you know, and the customer knows you understand, answer the question. Then, re-direct the customer's attention to gather more information about his or her full set of needs and deepen insight and understanding of those needs.

Instead of either interrogating the customer or simply relinquishing control over the sales process, there are effective approaches for re-direction and getting to a discussion of needs. In the easiest re-direction approach, answer the customer's question, show you have expertise, and establish credibility. Then, explain you would like to ask the customer a question in turn.

Explain why you would like to know more about the customer's needs. This could include telling the customer any of the following:

- You don't want to recommend the wrong solution. It's your intention to fully understand his or her needs in order to recommend the right solution. You simply need to know more in order to make the right recommendation.

- Your company has a huge selection of different versions of the product or service the customer is shopping for, and you want to supply the best choice.

- You want to determine if your company has the best solution for the customer's needs or if he or she would be better talking to some other supplier.

Then, ask permission to ask questions – about what the customer will be using the item for, or about what the customer is trying to accomplish.

The simple approach works and you could use it as your preferred style. However, you could be even more effective using a sophisticated re-direction. You can respond to customer questions using this process:

- agree with the importance of the question,

- clarify the underlying meaning of the question (*paraphrase*),

- answer the question,

- explain your intention to understand the customer's needs, and

- ask a situation or expectation question.

You come across as a more impressive insight-oriented consultant when you agree, clarify, answer, explain and then ask. You meet the customer right in his or her moment, and then take control of the conversation to lead it into Step Three – Take the Time to Learn The Customer's Needs (Get His Or Her S.P.I.C.E^3).

TOUGH CUSTOMERS

Some people are a real challenge. However, your success depends on being able to sell to these customers as well. It's your job to get past any roadblocks the customer puts in the way of engagement and get into an effective conversation about his or her S.P.I.C.E^3. Ask yourself, "What can I do to be the one who gets that sale?" And then, find the answer.

Where ever possible, use the following strategies:

- **Persist** – hang in there, don't just back off when the customer tries to distance him or herself from you.

- **Align yourself with the customer** – validate and identify with the customer's feelings, thoughts and needs.

- **Meet the customer in his or her moment** – answer any direct questions asked by the customer and agree with his or her concern.

- **Show empathy** – paraphrase what the customer says and reach for full understanding.

- **Use humour** – diffuse any tension between the customer and yourself with eye contact, a smile, and a humorous reply.

- **Establish expertise** – say things to show you know your stuff and can address the customer's needs.

- **If necessary, cause some doubt** – suggest that there may be more to think about than just what the customer is presenting as questions or statements.

- **Explain your intentions** – indicate you would like to ask some questions, explain why, and ask permission to do so.

- **Ask S.P.I.C.E[3] questions** – ask a question to learn what the customer wants to do with the product, and then ask again if the customer doesn't freely volunteer information.

DEALING WITH GRUFF/BELLIGERENT CUSTOMERS

For customers who are gruff in their responses to you – curt, offering non-verbal signals that suggest they won't be very cooperative, maybe even making statements to you that feel like criticism, use the powers of perseverance and patience. Don't just back off or quit. Use a comeback that catches the customer's attention.

For a retail example:

C: "Look. I'm just browsing." (*said with a touch of irritation*)

S: "Well, that's okay. We have a lot to browse. What are you browsing for?" (*makes eye contact and smiles*)

Or for a corporate example:

C: "You know, we're pretty happy with our current supplier." (*said with irritation*)

S: "I'm glad for you and your business. I'd hate to think our delay in asking to meet with you left you with a less than satisfactory supplier. Actually, I'm not after the business you send their way. I think there are other ways we can be helpful." (*makes eye contact and smiles*)

If the customer isn't already throwing you out of his or her office or walking away from you on the retail floor, persevere, use patience, stay calm, have a bit of a playful smile on your face and relish the challenge.

You could explain your positive intent, and then agree this might not seem appropriate to the customer right now. Make solid eye contact where ever possible and show confidence and respect for the customer. For example:

"Sounds like I hit a nerve, and this is a particularly bad time to talk with you about your concerns with XXXXXX?" (*Pause to wait for an answer while making eye contact and holding a bit of a smile*)

DEALING WITH A CUSTOMER WHO IS CRITICAL OF YOUR ABILITY TO BE HELPFUL,

If the customer challenges your expertise or ability to be helpful, you could agree then just proceed to ask what the customer is looking for. Alternatively, you could make statements or ask questions that demonstrate your confidence or expertise.

"That might be true. Tell me what kinds of products you're looking for and what you'll be doing with them."

or

"Possibly, but given my own experience using different versions of this XXXXXX, I may be able to help. We have several options that could potentially fit. Tell me more about what you will be doing with this XXXXXX."

Instead of arguing with the customer, invite the customer to show off his or her own technical knowledge. Then assert your own comfort in having a conversation about the needs the customer presents.

Remain calm and simply meet whatever response the customer gives you with a persistent intention to make sure the customer buys the proper solutions for his or her needs.

Paraphrase to be sure you understand what the customer is saying to you, then come back with both a form of agreement and a humorous reply while looking directly at the customer with a smile on your face. Give a playful response while making good eye contact. Maintain confidence that you can be helpful and offer real value. Explain your intentions. Hang in there.

DEALING WITH FEATURE SHOPPERS

Answer any question, then ask a question in turn. You might provide an answer that raises a concern. Create a bit of uncertainty in the mind of the customer by pointing out that the product could either not be enough to fully meet his or her needs, or it might be more than the customer needs. Be patient and persistent in trying to engage the customer in conversation, even when he or she just wants to talk product.

* * *

Build your skills for getting into conversations especially with "tough" customers. These are customers with whom everyone else is probably failing. They do buy, but on their own terms, wherever they find the best deal. Be the salesperson that gets conversational and learns their needs.

THE TRANSITION TO LEARNING THE NEEDS – GETTING THE S.P.I.C.E³

Once the person is engaged in a conversation with you, where he or she is willing to open up with you, steer the conversation to a discussion of the customer's needs. To do so, ask a transition question to move the focus on to what the customer is shopping for, or concerned about enough that he or she agreed to meet with you.

"So please tell me more about what you'll be using this XXXXXX for?"

or

"What concerns do you have about your current way of doing what you do?"

or

"What problems with your existing XXXXXX are causing you to look for a new one?"

or

"I'd like to understand your business better, particularly any issues you might be having where our firm could be of assistance. Can you tell me more about what your company does and how it does that work?"

or

"Please tell me about any business issues related to (*the product category*), where you're experiencing lower results than you think are possible?"

Remind the customer he or she had a purpose for coming into your store, or agreeing to meet with you. Your transition should lead right into that purpose.

STEP THREE – TAKE TIME TO LEARN THE NEEDS

(GET THE S.P.I.C.E³)

Before you ever recommend (or pitch) a product or service, know the customer's S.P.I.C.E³:

- *his or her situation,*

- *his or her problems,*

- *the implications of those problems,*

- *the constraints that have prevented problem solving before now, and*

- *his or her expectations and excitements about what he or she could achieve if those problems were solved.*

Otherwise, you could be selling the wrong things. And, if you know the S.P.I.C.E³, you won't be selling products. You'll be selling solutions.

Steer this conversation to an exploration of the customer's needs (his or her S.P.I.C.E^3). Endeavour to elevate your customer's insight about what has to change.

T	Take Time to Learn The Customer's Needs – Get the S.P.I.C.E^3.	Initiate an open discussion of the customer's needs to get his or her S.P.I.C.E^3, taking time to actively listen to the customer such that the customer does most of the talking while you clarify for understanding. Reach for deeper insight.

Conduct an effective and extensive diagnosis of the customer's needs, most particularly when the problems and related solutions are complex. This step is the primary step in our "GET SMARTER" sales process.

GOALS FOR STEP THREE – LEARNING THE CUSTOMER'S NEEDS

- Get the customer to trust you.

- Get the customer to tell you important information, some of which he or she might not have expected to share with you, and even some of which the customer hadn't even considered as relevant to solving his or her problems.

- Learn the customer's particular S.P.I.C.E^3.

- Take the customer through his or her Reality Trough, opening up the customer's awareness to the emotions that reside within that trough.

- Help the customer to achieve new insights.

- Work with the customer so you both achieve full understanding of the customer's needs.

- Build the customer's eagerness to hear what you have to recommend.

Gather information in a conversation as opposed to an interrogation. You want this conversation to feel good to the customer.

GET THE S.P.I.C.E^3

Situation	The customer's current situation; what he or she does; what he or she uses now; how he or she does it; why he or she does it; who will be the doer; under-utilized and potential resources within the situation.
Problems	The symptoms, difficulties, real problems, challenges, and opportunities the customer has when doing what he or she does; and what wishes he or she has to do it better.
Implications	What it costs the customer, tangibly and intangibly, to have these problems; and what feelings the customer has about these costs, including feelings about lost opportunities.
Constraints	Why the customer hasn't fixed these problems or concerns before now; what has blocked him or her from taking appropriate action; and which of these constraints are real impediments and not just imagined.
E^3 xpectations, excitement, and eagerness	What the customer would minimally expect to gain; what results would really excite the customer (*reduced costs, increased gain, new opportunities, better results and benefits*); and how eager the customer is to get the problem solved.

Learn all that you can about the customers S.P.I.C.E^3 because that is what matters to the customer. This is the full definition of the problem the customer wants to solve. See yourself as a problem solver. As such you must achieve a full understanding of the customer's problem before you can recommend the correct solution.

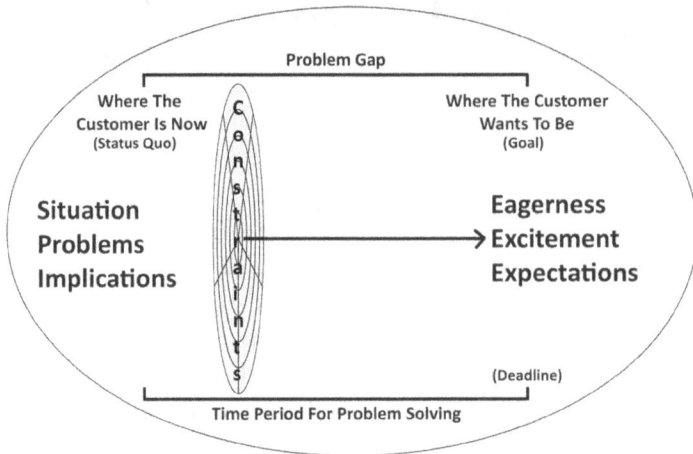

Recognize symptoms for clues to problems the customer might not yet fully appreciate. By asking about those symptoms, by searching out symptom origins, you may expand the customer's awareness as to the true nature of his or her problem(s).

Help the customer to address the implications of his or her problems so the reality becomes clearer to him or her. This will surface the feelings of frustration the customer has with his or her situation. This takes the customer into the emotions of the Reality Trough, and from that place, the motivation to find a better solution will begin to emerge.

Examine what reasons the customer thinks have kept him or her from solving the problems before now. These constraints become reasons not to buy. Induce the customer to consider whether or not these constraints are real or imagined. Know the real constraints so your recommended solution includes ways and means to overcome them.

Get the customer to share what he or she minimally expects, so you know the minimum standards the solution must meet. Also ask what benefits the customer would really like to achieve if a perfect solution could be found. A higher level of expectation is determined and you have a better target for what your solution must deliver.

Learn how eager the customer is to hear what you have to recommend. If the customer isn't feeling eager, he or she is likely to resist. Instead of resistance, the customer should be in a state of desire.

By opening up the conversation to discuss all of the elements of the customer's S.P.I.C.E[3], you nudge the customer from the comfort of his or her status quo toward his or her excitement about the benefits that could be realized. Stimulate the customer's eagerness to find a solution.

The following sample questions could be asked to uncover each of the five elements. After your greeting and engagement, start with a situation question.

SITUATION QUESTIONS

Gather data and facts about the customer's status quo. Determine if this is a likely environment for the problems your solution will solve. In addition, help the customer to better know his or her situation and the resources within it.

- Can you tell me what you'll be using an XXXXXX for?

- You know your current situation better than I do. Please tell me as much as you can about how you do what you do where you think a new XXXXXX would be helpful?

- What have you been using up till now?

- Who will be using this XXXXXX?

- How did you do that before now?

- Are there any particular resources within your situation now that we should be thinking about as we consider how to be of assistance?

Situation Insight Potential – *Explore how the customer sees, hears, feels, understands his or her current environment. Expand the customer's awareness of what is pertinent in his or her status quo. Help the customer to discover previously undervalued resources within the current situation that might be useful when a new solution is identified.*

All situations have some problems within them. If the customer isn't giving you clues about such problems, you might have to ask a question or two to direct the customer to tell you what you need to know.

PROBLEM QUESTIONS

Ask these questions to discover the symptoms, difficulties, dissatisfactions, real problems, challenges and opportunities the customer is having in his or her current situation. Cause the customer to see his or her problem(s) differently and to realize problems he or she didn't know existed, or to see new opportunities he or she hadn't yet considered.

- What don't you like about the way you currently do things?

- If you were to say your current way of doing things could be improved, what would you improve?

- What problems with your current XXXXXX cause you to think about getting a new one?

- What frustrations do you have with your current XXXXXX that cause you to look for a new one?

- We've noticed that some of our customers experience (*typical symptoms of the problem your solution resolves*). Have any of these symptoms been evident in your situation?

- How often do you encounter (*typical symptoms of the problem your solution resolves*)?

- Given changes in your environment, are new opportunities presenting themselves?

- Are there any things you would like to be able to do that you can't do now?

Focus the customer's awareness on symptoms, the real cause of the symptoms, and new opportunities.

> ***Problem Insight Potential*** *– Convert "assumed to be just normal" attributes of the client's situation into perceived symptoms of a problem that needs to be resolved and not just accepted. Expose the real problem when that problem has not previously been understood. In addition, expand the customer's awareness of neglected opportunities.*

If the customer does not have any of the problems that your solutions solve, diplomatically end your sales interaction. If possible, make a referral to someone who may have the correct solution.

Where the customer has problems for which you have solutions, you next want the customer to quantify the costs of his or her problems, both tangible and intangible costs as much as possible. In doing so, he or she will encounter whatever emotions he or she has about these costs.

If the customer hasn't yet given you clues about the implications, you will have to ask an implication-oriented question to steer the conversation in that direction.

IMPLICATION QUESTIONS

Specifically discover the degree of quantifiable cost, frustration, and pain the customer has within his or her status quo.

- What are the real costs of these symptoms and problems?

- What does it cost you when you can't do what you want to do with your current XXXXXX?

- If things aren't working as well as you would like, what does it cost you to stick with the status quo?

- Sometimes there are hidden costs doing things the way we do them now. Are there any you can identify?

- Are there any intangible costs, such as the sense things aren't as good as they could be, complaints and the dissatisfaction of others, morale issues, quality being less than you would like, emotional costs such as disappointment or frustration?

- Has this problem held you back in any way from achieving your goals and targets?

- Are you experiencing any of the following costs:
  - costs of error or failure,
  - downtime costs,
  - growing maintenance costs,
  - lost opportunities,

- o   negative impact on others, or

- o   costs of delay ?

- I assume you have new opportunities you aren't yet able to pursue. What benefits and improved results might you be missing by not pursuing such new opportunities? What does that ultimately cost you?

Know the financial implications – the dollar costs your customer has to deal with. This information will determine the value of what the customer will ultimately choose to buy. The customer's motivation will rise if he or she concludes these costs are no longer acceptable.

> ***Implication Insight Potential*** *– Deliver new insights as the customer measures the full costs of his or her problems. He or she will likely realize that the consequences of not taking action are too great to live with or accept any longer. Help the customer to discover costs that hadn't previously been considered or fully understood.*

After realizing that the costs are greater than first thought, the customer might hesitate as he or she bumps up against what stops him or her from solving the problems. The conversation now needs to focus on what is preventing a solution.

CONSTRAINT QUESTIONS

Ask constraint-focused questions to find out what the customer thinks is blocking him or her from solving the problem(s).

- Could you please tell me about the constraints that hold you back from getting this problem solved?

- What stopped you from making this change before today?

- Are any roadblocks preventing you from making improvements?

- Various things keep us from upgrading. What are your reasons for sticking it out this long?

- What alternatives have you already tried or considered, and what prevented them from producing your desired outcomes?

- If your problem persists despite your best efforts, you must be bumping up against some tough roadblocks. What are they?

- Given that you've examined various alternative solutions, can you tell me why you've rejected each of them as unworkable in your situation?

- There are likely some pretty important criteria that any solution must meet. Please tell me what they are and why you think they are so critical.

Part of the exploration of constraints would include a determination as to the reality of these constraints. Are they real or imagined?

- Of the roadblocks you've identified, which ones most significantly get in your way?

- Sometimes we think a constraint really prevents our taking action, but when we examine it, we realize it's something we can work around. Does this apply to any that you've just listed?

- If you had to prioritize the constraints in terms of their importance, what constraints would be the most important and which constraints are less limiting?

- There are times when we limit our own ability to make changes. Thinking about the constraints you've identified, are any of them just excuses you're in the habit of using to keep from making a change, and not real roadblocks?

- As you consider them, which of these constraints is a real roadblock and which might just be an imagined limitation?

Constraints Insight Potential – *This conversation helps to identify what is truly blocking change and what are only self imposed or imagined limitations. As this is clarified, the client is enabled to make a choice for change based on the reality of his or her situation. The customer gets to challenge his or her assumptions about what really does prevent change. In turn, the customer's information informs the salesperson as to the full set of requirements the solution must satisfy.*

Once you discover what has prevented action before now, shift to an exploration of what might be possible if the constraints were removed and the problems solved. Discover what the customer would expect to gain if the best possible solution could be developed. Start that process with one of these E^3 questions.

EXPECTATIONS, EXCITEMENT, EAGERNESS (E^3) QUESTIONS

Discover what benefits your customer is looking to buy, and how eager he or she is to experience those benefits.

- What do you think the benefits would be if you could solve this problem?

- So what do you hope to gain the most with this new XXXXXX?

- What benefits would you like to be able to achieve that you can't experience now?

- What are your minimum expectations for the results you would have to achieve if you get a new XXXXXX?

- If you could get everything you wanted, what would be the most important gain for you?

- If a miracle could occur overnight, what would you be able to do tomorrow that you can't do right now, and what would be the benefits you could see happening because of this?

- If we were able to come up with a solution that exceeded all of the expectations you've had up until now, what extra benefits would you really like to achieve?

- What do you think would be the most exciting benefit of getting a new XXXXXX?

- When do you hope to have the new XXXXXX in place?

- How eager do you think you are to achieve these benefits?

- How long do you think you can wait before a new solution is put in place?

Expectation/Excitements/Eagerness (E³) Insight Potential –
Help the customer to clarify his or her minimum requirements
that any solution must meet. Then elevate the customer's
expectations. Bring about a new energy and desire for greater
benefits. Instill an eagerness to discover how improvement
can be achieved. Shift the customer from hesitation and
resistance to a desire for action. Determine if there are any
deadlines the customer hadn't previously considered.

* * *

When the customer learns something new and important as a result of his or her conversation with you, you substantially differentiate yourself from any other salesperson that just tries to sell his or her stuff.

We presented examples of questions for each of the five S.P.I.C.E³ elements. Ask one or at most two questions for each element of the S.P.I.C.E³ conversation. Use only a question or two to get that aspect of the conversation going. Too many questions feels like an interrogation. Instead, you should be primarily listening to the customer as he or she shares this information with you during this step in the sales process.

Use these questions to start the exploration of each element then use the active listening skills to draw out deeper information. Know how and when to ask just a few to get your customer sharing the important answers with you. Learn all this information, not by questions, but by getting conversational. Don't interrogate.

Your goal is to reach for **full understanding**. You achieve full understanding through the process of listening to the customer, reflecting back what you understand from what the customer has said to you, and checking to see if you have understood. You achieve full understanding when this active listening process causes the customer to gain new insights about his or her problems, implications, constraints and desired achievements.

ACHIEVING FULL UNDERSTANDING

Achieve all three of the important aspects of full understanding. It is not enough to achieve just one or two of them. You both must understand more deeply than before the S.P.I.C.E^3 conversation and both must know that you understand.

FULL UNDERSTANDING =

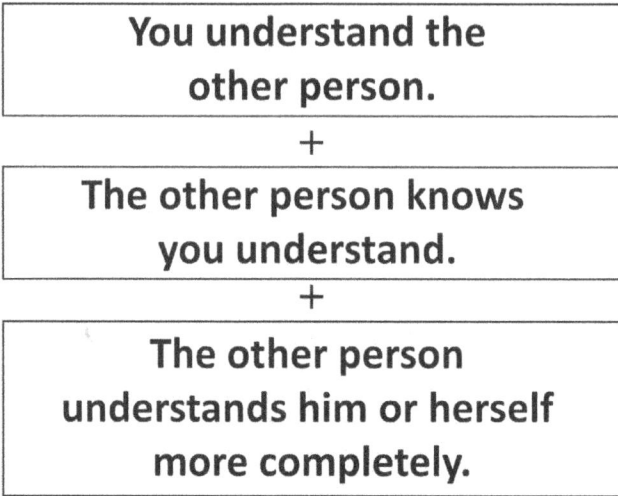

> ### You understand the
> ### other person.

$+$

> ### The other person knows
> ### you understand.

$+$

> ### The other person
> ### understands him or herself
> ### more completely.

First, understand the customer. Secondly, show the customer that you understand by presenting back to the customer what you think you're getting and check to make sure you've understood. Lastly, increase the customer's understanding of his or her own needs as the customer sees and hears him or herself more completely through what you reflect back.

ACTIVE LISTENING SKILLS

Use particular active listening skills to learn the customer's full S.P.I.C.E^3 without doing an interrogation.

INVITATIONS

An invitation is a specific request for the customer to tell you something about him or herself.

"Please tell me more about…"

or

"That's Interesting, I sure would like to know more."

Explained Invitations

Alternatively, first explain why you want to know more, and then invite the customer to tell you.

Explained Invitations

A statement of the importance of the information you need in order to better understand.

$+$

An invitation to tell you more and give you more information

"That sounds important and might influence which product is the right one for you. Could you please tell me more about that?"

or

"It's critical that I understand the real problem you're trying to solve by buying a new solution today. You've said you have a problem with your _____. Please tell me more about how you experience this issue?"

Make it easier for the customer to understand your intent and to give you more information.

Paraphrasing

Paraphrasing is the act of sharing what you think the other person means and then asking if you have understood correctly. Give the other person a chance to correct you so he or she can expand on what is being said.

You check to see if you have understood the customer's full meaning. You don't just listen passively to his or her words. You interpret the meaning first and then you reflect back your interpretation and ask if it is correct.

Paraphrasing

> **A statement that shows what you think the other person meant by what he or she said (your interpretation of the meaning of the other person's words).**

$$+$$

> **A check-out question to determine if you have understood correctly.**

"I think you're saying that....   Am I understanding you?"

or

"It seems like you mean....   Am I right?"

or

"From what you've said,
I'm guessing you mean....   Correct?"

Reflect back the full interpretation of what you get so the other person can correct you if you don't understand properly. Don't just repeat back what the customer said. Instead, you share your interpretation and ask if you have interpreted accurately.

There is almost always a gap between what the other person says and what we think he or she means. Your interpretation could:

- match what the other person intended to convey in the way of meaning,

- be close but not quite what the other person meant,

- be completely inaccurate, or

- be more than the other person intended but still accurate.

So we have to check to see if we have interpreted correctly. The customer can then do one of four things:

- Acknowledge the accuracy of your understanding – "Yes, that's what I meant."

- Correct the inaccuracy of your understanding – "No what I meant is …."

- Expand on the accuracy of your understanding – "Yes I mean that and also …"

- Acknowledge your accuracy and expand on his or her own thinking – "Yes and that reminds me, I…"

Any of these responses leads you to full understanding because the information is clarified and expanded for both of you.

INFERENCE CHECKING

Use your natural tendency to form impressions about the other person based on the information he or she gives or shows and find out if the guesses you make about this other person are accurate.

Inference Checking

A statement telling the other person what you infer or guess about him or her based on what you have seen or heard from the other person or have heard about him or her, or otherwise know about his or her context.

+

A check-out question to determine if your inference or guess is correct.

To check your inferences, tell the customer what you infer or guess about him or her then check to determine if your inferences are correct.

"I'm guessing you ....   Am I correct?"

or

"It's my inference that....   Is this right?"

or

"Perhaps you want...   Correct?"

Make positive assumptions about your customers and it will be easier for them to respond to your Inference Checks.

"Bill, you're in the trucking business, and similar clients have been very concerned about the rising costs of fuel additives. I'm guessing that applies to you as well?"

The customer can make any of the same four responses as he or she would in response to a paraphrase:

- acknowledge that you understand,

- correct you,

- acknowledge some understanding and expand, or

- acknowledge and add new information that was triggered by your check-out.

FEELINGS CHECKING

Listen to voice tone and tempo, watch for facial, body and hand gestures, notice what is said and not said. Get a sense of how the other person is feeling based on these observations. Make your guess about the underlying emotions.

State your guess as to how the customer is feeling, and ask if you have guessed correctly.

"I'm guessing you feel...   Am I understanding you?"

or

"It seems like you feel...   Am I right?"

or

"You're likely feeling...   Is this correct?"

Fill in the blank with an emotion word – emotion words like discouraged, excited, anxious, upset, eager, disappointed, confused, angry, frustrated, sad, appreciative, etc.

Feelings Checking

> A statement telling the other person what you infer or guess about the other person's feelings based on what you have seen or heard from the other person or know about his or her situation.

$+$

> A check-out question to determine if your inference or guess about the feelings is correct.

Once again, the customer can acknowledge that you're accurately reading his or her emotions, correct you, acknowledge some understanding and expand, or acknowledge and add new information stimulated by the customer's expanding awareness of his or her own feelings.

IDENTIFICATION

Show the other person you understand his or her situation either because you've been in a similar circumstance yourself, or you can at least imagine what it must feel like to be him or her. Show empathy.

Think of a time when you were in a similar predicament or imagine yourself in the other person's situation and check your own awareness of how you would feel. Then ask yourself, "How would I feel if this were me?"

"I remember when I bought my first XXXXXX. I felt lost and confused about the many technical words I'd never heard before. I guess you feel the same way right now. Correct?"

or

"If I imagine myself in your situation, having just realized how much I'm currently paying for less than satisfactory results, I'd feel disappointed about not having had this fixed earlier. Are you feeling that way?"

Identification

> **Your description of your own similar experience and the feelings that you had, or your guess about how you would feel if you were in the same situation as the other person is experiencing.**

$+$

> **A check-out question to determine if the other person feels the same way.**

EFFECTIVE QUESTIONING

Ask different types of questions. Open questions solicit larger answers. Exploratory questions seek elaboration and an expanded story. There are different types of useful open and exploratory questions.

- **Standard Questions** start with who, what, where, when, how, and why. A standard question is an open question seeking an elaborate answer. When you ask, "How do you do this now, given that you don't have a XXXXXX yet?", you're asking a standard question.

- **Status Quo Questions** try to get an elaboration of the customer's current situation. For example, you could ask, "How is your day-to-day work affected by your current XXXXXX?"

- The **"Best Of All Possible Worlds" Questions** ask the customer to imagine the best possibility and describe what that would look like. For example, you could ask, "If a new XXXXXX could give you a competitive advantage, what would the advantage be?"

- **Assumptive Questions** start with a positive assumption about the customer then finish with a question that relates to that assumption. For example, you could ask, "When you measured the costs of that problem, what did you discover?" or "When you asked your people to solve that issue, what happened?" or "When you did…, what took place?"

- **Multiple Choice Questions** help your customer to answer a question by giving him or her several answers to choose from. For example, "When choosing their delivery supplier, some people are more concerned about delivery costs than the time of delivery, the method of delivery, or the tracking of the delivery. Which is most important to you?"

or

- **Explained Questions** give the other person a reference point to better understand the reason for giving you the information. Explain why you wish to ask the question. For example, you could say, "In order to make a proper recommendation, I need to know what you'll be using the XXXXXX for and what you hope to gain by using it. What benefits are you looking for?"

Being questioned too much can feel uncomfortable, like being interrogated. Know:

- when to ask a question,

- what to ask about,

- how to choose the type of question to ask in order to make answering the question easier for the customer, and

- when to use the active listening skills instead.

MATCHING

If you really want to build rapport with another person, if you really want to show you understand, if you really want to get into the other person's shoes to achieve full understanding, then subtly and gently adopt some of the gestures, posture, voice tone and tempo, eye movement patterns, and words and phrases used by the other person. The key word is "subtle". Match enough but not too much.

USING THE ACTIVE LISTENING SKILLS

Don't move on to selling your products and services until you fully understand the customer's needs. Half of the time available with this customer should be spent on the first three steps. Take the time to "GET" the information you need in order to make an effective recommendation.

Start with a Situation Question to learn more about what the customer is trying to do. Keep the customer talking by actively following what the customer says. Reflect back what you receive from the customer so the customer can correct you if you misunderstand, or further elaborate if you do understand.

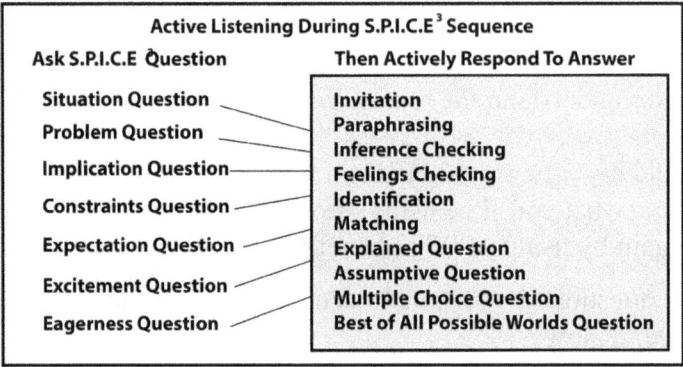

Active Listening During S.P.I.C.E^3 Sequence	
Ask S.P.I.C.E Question	Then Actively Respond To Answer
Situation Question	Invitation
Problem Question	Paraphrasing
	Inference Checking
Implication Question	Feelings Checking
Constraints Question	Identification
	Matching
Expectation Question	Explained Question
Excitement Question	Assumptive Question
	Multiple Choice Question
Eagerness Question	Best of All Possible Worlds Question

Pay attention to the customer's non-verbal behaviour as well as to what the customer says, because these can be important clues about the customer's feelings. Use the feelings checking skill to make sure you read the customer's emotions correctly, and to show respect for those feelings. Use the skill of identification with the customer to show empathy, and to help the customer feel safe in talking about him or herself.

Continue through each of the five elements. Focus on a particular element by starting with a question appropriate to that element then clarify with the active listening skills until you know what you need to know about that element. Then ask a question for the next element in the S.P.I.C.E^3.

Once the customer has elaborated as much as possible in response to your use of the active listening skills, ask a few questions to get the remaining bits of information you need to know. Use explained, assumptive, multiple choice, and "best of all possible world" questions.

Do your best to move through the five components in the order of S.P.I.C.E[3] so the customer feels the lows of having unsolved problems and finishes the conversation feeling the highs of what it might be like if those problems were solved.

Behaviours That Get In The Way

Guard yourself from using certain behaviours that get in the way of listening.

- **Pitching Your Product** – offering information about your products, services, and solutions in response to something the customer has just said.

- **Listening For Just The Facts** – focusing so much on the facts that the position, ideas, or emotions that the facts are intended to convey are missed.

- **Not Taking Notes** – relying on memory, which gets harder to do when the story gets more complex, and consequently important parts of the story are forgotten.

- **Distractions** – putting up with or causing distractions like the clicking of a pen, talking with someone else while the speaker is talking, or doing something else while listening

- **Emotional Distractions** – having specific feelings in response to something the speaker says that trigger thoughts of prior situations, taking your attention away from what is being communicated.

- **Preconceptions** – not listening to what the customer says because of some preconceived idea (*i.e. hearing something that makes you think he or she is just like other customers*).

- **Embarrassment** – missing something the speaker said and being too embarrassed to ask him or her to repeat it, or being too intimidated to give back your interpretation out of fear that you are wrong.

- **Interruptions** – cutting off or otherwise interrupting the speaker because you think you have something more important to say or ask.

- **Premature Directive Questions** – cutting off the flow of the customer's story by asking a pointed or direct question that changes the subject and directs the customer to attend to what you think is important before the customer has had a chance to tell you what he or she thinks is most important.

- **Criticizing** – privately thinking about or publicly commenting on negative aspects of the speaker or what he or she is telling you instead of learning his or her full meaning.

- **Faking Attention Or Rehearsing** – thinking of something other than what the customer is saying, or mentally preparing what to say next, or thinking about your next question.

- **Prejudging** – adopting a negative attitude and tuning the speaker out (*for example, by deciding they probably won't buy much*).

NOT ABOUT PRODUCTS – IT'S ABOUT THE S.P.I.C.E³

Have a self-imposed rule against talking about product or solutions at this stage. Don't ask questions about which products the customer wants, likes or needs, or even which features the customer wants, likes or needs. Steer the conversation away from a product focus if you can, to a focus on what the person, or the corporation wants to accomplish with the products.

YOUR OWN COMFORT WITH FEELINGS

Bringing the implications of the status quo into full awareness will surface negative emotions along with the realization that the costs are higher than the person was admitting to him or herself. Assist the feelings to surface and the motivation to change will rise. These skills make it easier for the other person to listen to your recommendation when it is time for you to make it.

WHEN SELLING TO ORGANIZATIONS, GROUPS OR FAMILIES

If you frequently sell to corporations, groups or families, you will have to find out ways to learn about the S.P.I.C.E³ of all people who will participate in decision-making and those who will be most significantly impacted by the changes arising from implementation of a new solution. The first half of the selling process will be longer as you speak to each V.I.P. involved in the purchase process.

As you move from person to person, identify the problems from each person's perspective then find out how each person experiences the implications and constraints. Learn what each person would ideally like to see as results when a new solution is applied.

WHEN TO MOVE TO THE NEXT STEP

Move forward when you have indications from the customer that you fully understand him or her, and that the customer now understands his or her own needs better. You are particularly ready if the customer has achieved new insights about his or her needs and is very eager to find a solution. Its time to move to the next step if you hear the customer say, "Thank you for helping me clarify my needs. What do you recommend?"

Decide whether to follow getting your customer's S.P.I.C.E³ with either Option 1 – moving to half time where you use a break in the interaction to prepare for your summary and your recommendation, or Option 2 – summarizing what you've learned before half time, or Option 3 – doing the summary of your customer's S.P.I.C.E³ both before and after half time. Use your judgment in each situation to determine which option to utilize.

The decision depends on how clearly both of you understand the customer's S.P.I.C.E³, how deeply the customer has felt his or her Reality Trough, and how eager the customer is to receive your recommendation. It also depends on how long Half Time is going to be. Following a long Half Time, do the summary again even if you did it before.

Option 1 Half Time Before Summary	Option 2 Summary Before Half Time	Option 3 Before and After Half Time
Greet	Greet	Greet
Engage	Engage	Engage
Take Time To Learn The Customer's S.P.I.C.E^3	Take Time To Learn The Customer's S.P.I.C.E^3	Take Time To Learn The Customer's S.P.I.C.E^3
Half Time	Show Full Understanding - Summarize The S.P.I.C.E^3	Show Full Understanding - Summarize The S.P.I.C.E^3
Show Full Understanding - Summarize The S.P.I.C.E^3	*Half Time*	*Half Time*
Make Your Recommendation	Make Your Recommendation	Summarize The S.P.I.C.E^3 Again
		Make Your Recommendation

THE TRANSITION TO HALF TIME

Use Half Time to prepare yourself for the second half of the sales process. Ask for time away from the client to do your preparation.

"I think I have an understanding of your needs and expectations. If you agree, I'd like just a few minutes (*hours, days, weeks*) to prepare my recommendation. If you're okay with the wait, perhaps you could (*complete this credit application while you wait; or conduct an investigation as to the costs of the problems we identified in case we haven't fully assessed them; or read this information to help you determine what to consider when making your decision*). Is that okay with you?"

If you've made the decision to break for Half Time, you want your client waiting with anticipation for what you'll bring back as your solution.

THE TRANSITION TO SHOW FULL UNDERSTANDING

On the other hand, if your needs-assessment conversation hasn't been as organized as it could have been and the customer needs to have a clear description of his or her S.P.I.C.E^3 along with a chance to more deliberately review the emotions of his or her Reality Trough, you need a way to transition to a summary of what you learned. Tell your customer you think you understand what he or she needs, and then ask for permission to summarize what you've just learned to confirm understanding.

"Before I make my recommendation, I want to be completely sure I fully understand. I'd like to summarize what you've told me. Is that okay? "

If okay, transition to Step Four and summarize his or her S.P.I.C.E^3 clearly taking your customer through the Reality Trough.

HALF TIME

(GETTING READY TO MAKE YOUR RECOMMENDATION)

Half time can be as short as a few seconds while you gather your thoughts, or as long as six months if the solution isn't yet available. The client will wait as long as it takes – if you've done the first half effectively.

During Half Time, review your own understanding of the customer's needs, determine the right solution for those needs, prepare to present your solution, and if necessary, rehearse how you will summarize to show full understanding before you make your recommendation.

G	Greet	Greet and approach showing interest in the customer and beginning a conversation.
E	Engage	Engage in conversation allowing relationship building to occur.
T	Take Time to Learn the Customer's Needs (Get The Customer's S.P.I.C.E^3)	Get the S.P.I.C.E^3 in an open discussion of the customer's needs, reaching for new insights and taking time to actively listen to the customer as the customer does most of the talking while you clarify for understanding (*reach for deeper insight*).
	Half Time	*Identify the best solution, prepare to recommend your complete package of products and services, and if necessary, rehearse how you will summarize the customer's S.P.I.C.E^3 to show full understanding.*

GOALS OF HALF TIME

- Acquire the expertise (*either on your own or by turning to in-house or supplier-based experts*) that allows you to determine the best solution for the customer's needs.

- Determine if you have a solution that fully satisfies the customer's needs.

- Locate all of the components of that complete solution.

- Prepare to make your recommendation.

and

- If you have initiated Half Time before doing the summary of the customer's S.P.I.C.E^3, then prepare to return with an organized summary that will take the customer through his or her Reality Trough.

Half Time emphasizes that half of the time normally spent with a client would be spent getting critical information to effectively determine what to sell.

THE DURATION OF HALF TIME

The time you take will depend on the complexity of the customer's needs, what you sell, your knowledge of your solution options, the problems each option can solve, and who you're selling to. Decide if you are just going to tell your customer what you recommend, present a written proposal or quote, gather up all the components that make up the solution to show to the customer, or make an in-action demonstration of your solution.

In turn, the customer's needs may determine the length of Half Time. Make sure the Half Time interval works for both you and your customer.

THE SALESPERSON

DETERMINE IF YOU CAN SOLVE THE PROBLEM

Determine if you actually have a solution that best meets the customer's full set of needs. Your solution must truly satisfy all constraints and fully realize the results and benefits the client expects to achieve. If you are not able to do this, you will have to return to the customer and make this declaration.

IDENTIFY THE SOLUTION

Determine which mix of products and services best solve this customer's unique problem(s). However, in some situations, the customer's problems may require a more complex customized solution.

When selling large-scale custom solutions, Half Time will involve significant problem-solving activity and require more time. Meet with any of your company's technical experts, potential suppliers, your sales manager and your sales team to have a creative discussion that leads to an innovative solution. Determine:

- What can we combine with our existing product(s) to make a workable solution?

- How could we easily re-engineer our solutions so they have the abilities required by the customer?

- How could our products be implemented with under-utilized resources already owned by the client to produce the desired results?

- What changes could we make to our ordering processes, inventory management, packaging, quantity requirements, delivery, financing, warranty, maintenance services, installation schedule, mix of products, or end of life services to make our solutions more acceptable to the customer?

- What could we remove from the problem situation to make our solution appropriate?

- Who has complimentary products and services we can bundle with our own to provide an effective solution?

- Is there a supplier we don't usually buy from that might have the solution this customer requires?

- Is there a manufacturer that might be interested in working with us to produce a solution that will meet this customer's needs?

- How can we share the risk of a new solution with the customer – delayed payment structures, loaned personnel, rental as opposed to sale, or immediate product replacement if failure?

LOCATE THE SOLUTION

Do what you have to do in order to locate the source of supply for the best solution and determine its availability.

DEVELOP THE SOLUTION

Often complete solutions require partnerships and alliances. Form a partnership with other providers to create the complete solution that meets the customer's needs.

Quotes And Proposals

For many customers, you may be required to develop a comprehensive proposal. This formal document should be a professional quality document. Write effectively and get others to check your work.

Write a comprehensive proposal or quote when:

- the customer stipulates that such a written proposal is required to satisfy the customer's buying process,

- the customer is making a complicated purchase to solve a serious problem,

- the customer has to get buying approval from a committee of decision makers, or

- you're doing a consultation for a business to solve a comprehensive business problem.

For Retail Sales

For the retail customer that requests a quotation, prepare a one or two page quote which includes:

- the customer's S.P.I.C.E[3] emphasizing the insights your customer achieved, particularly regarding the problem, implications, constraints, and the most exciting benefits.

- a description of the solution which could include all of the elements of the solution in a list, but without line item pricing.

- a clear description of the benefits to be realized by this solution.

- the total price and the recommended payment strategy such as financing, leasing or staged pricing based on the installation period.

- a summary of the net gains the customer will realize.

- a description of what would happen after the customer decides to buy.

- an indication of your eagerness to earn your customer's business.

and,

- an indication you will call to follow-up at a specific date and time.

For Corporate And Possibly Outbound Sales

Essentially, the proposal for a large potential sale would read like a summary of the selling process:

- an executive summary (*which contains a brief description of what follows in the rest of the quote or proposal*),

- an expression of appreciation for the chance to submit a proposal,

- a description of the customer's S.P.I.C.E[3] making sure to include the information that emerged as insights during your conversation(s) with your customer,

  o a brief but hi-light description of the customer's situation,

  o a description of the symptoms, problems and unrealized opportunities the customer has in the situation,

  o a description of the implications or consequences of those problems (*as numerically as possible*),

  o a description of what the customer identified as reasons why he or she hasn't changed before now (*the constraints the customer faces*),

  o a description of the results, benefits, payoffs, expectations and excitements the customer hopes to realize by finding a solution to his or her problem(s),

- a description of your recommended solution, listing all of the components of your complete solution,

- a list of the benefits your solution will provide, detailing financial benefits where possible, and covering all of the benefits the client expects to achieve,

- a clear price for the total solution (*you could place the price for each element of your solution in an appendix if this is required by the client, but we suggest not doing so if not required*),

- a comparison of this price to any financial value or gain that would result from implementing your solution, in such a way that it's very clear the value exceeds price,

- a description of how this investment can be financed for the customer's benefit,

- a detailed listing of the implementation process once the decision is made to purchase, showing time frames, activities, and person's responsible,

- a clear indication of the next step in the buying process, such as a call by you to follow-up the proposal at a set time,

- a list of reasons why a client would benefit by buying from your firm,

- an appendix with:

  o copies of letters of reference from clients who had similar problems solved by your products and services,

  o a clear description of any alliances formed to provide this solution,

  o any technical literature that would help the client evaluate the solution you've proposed,

  o any critical information that demonstrates the ability of your company to provide this solution, such as details about key personnel in the company, any public financial information showing the success of your company, and letters from suppliers showing you are a valued part of their product chain.

Place the word "Confidential" in the header or footer of each page and insert something like the following sentence on the proposal cover.

"The information, ideas and format contained in this proposal are the confidential property of (*name of your company*) and should not be disclosed to any individual who does not work for (*name of your client*) and specifically not to any competitor of (*name of your company*)."

Build a template to be used for other proposals for other customers as this makes the process faster and easier. Have someone else read your proposal before submission. Present the proposal personally and give an executive summary before handing it over. Ask the customer if assistance is needed in making the presentation to any other decision makers. Ask for feedback on your proposal after the customer has made the decision.

PREPARE YOUR S.P.I.C.E^3 SUMMARY

If you intend to return from Half Time to do "Step Four – Show Full Understanding", you need to organize what you know about your customer's S.P.I.C.E^3, and prepare to make a summary presentation of that S.P.I.C.E^3 once you return to the customer. Rehearse what you will say so you can take the customer into the lows of the Reality Trough and the highs of the E^3 expected gain.

THE CLIENT

Assign some related activity that prepares the customer for the next step. For example, the client could:

- view a video demo,

- contact other customers who have purchased from you,

- watch a fully automated PowerPoint presentation,

- fill out a credit application,

- read materials to increase his or her expertise as a buyer,

- talk with others who will be influenced by the buying decision,

- find out if others have additional information to clarify the S.P.I.C.E^3,

- get detailed costs of the problems to heighten motivation to get a solution, or

- arrange to get others to come to a meeting with you to receive your proposal.

WHEN TO MOVE OUT OF HALF TIME

Move out of Half Time when you're ready to make a recommendation and the customer is ready to receive it. Transition out of Half Time to revive your customer's eagerness by going to "Step Four – Show Full Understanding"; or, out of Half Time to "Step Five – Make the Recommendation"; or, out of Half Time to provide some indication as to how long it will take to have the best solution available to the client. Alternatively, if you are not able to provide one, you will have to return to the customer and make this declaration.

TRANSITION FROM HALF TIME WHEN YOU DON'T HAVE A SOLUTION

If you do not have the best solution available at this time, you will have to do one of the following:

- refer the customer to a supplier that does have the solution,

- indicate that you need more time to find the solution because the solution isn't readily available, but you have some ideas where to find it, or

- indicate that the solution does not yet exist and that you will contact the customer as soon as it is available.

"Jill, I was so excited about finding the best solution for your needs but my technical experts have advised me that what is available on the market at this time doesn't yet do what you need. We suggest you wait and get the solution that does meet your needs. I'll watch for such a solution and contact you as soon as I know it's available. Is that okay with you?"

TRANSITION FROM HALF TIME TO MAKE THE RECOMMENDATION

Ask the customer if he or she is ready to hear your recommendation then present what you prepared during half time by moving to "Step Five – Make Your Recommendation".

"Thank you for this second meeting. I met with our specialists and we've come up with a solution that reduces your costs and increases your profitability. I'm excited about how this can make a difference to your bottom-line, and relatively quickly. Shall we proceed?"

TRANSITION TO SHOW FULL UNDERSTANDING

Return to the customer and ask permission to summarize, explaining that you want to make sure you fully understand the customer's needs.

"Thank you for waiting. I think I've found a great solution for your needs. Before I show it to you, I would like to refresh both of our memories by reviewing what we discussed in our last meeting. Is that okay with you?"

STEP FOUR – SHOW FULL UNDERSTANDING

(SUMMARIZE WHAT YOU'VE LEARNED ABOUT THE CUSTOMER'S S.P.I.C.E³)

In this step, take the customer through his or her Reality Trough. Summarize what you've learned about:

- *his or her situation,*

- *his or her problems,*

- *the implications of those problems,*

- *what has stopped the customer from finding a solution before now, and*

- *what he or she will gain by solving his or her problems.*

This should highlight the customer's new insights and involve a movement through the emotions of the Reality Trough arriving at excitement, anticipation, and eagerness.

Before trying to sell anything, you summarize what you've learned about the customer's needs and expectations, and ask if you have fully understood.

GOALS OF STEP FOUR – SHOW FULL UNDERSTANDING

- Prove to yourself you've achieved full understanding of your customer's S.P.I.C.E[3.]

- Prove to the customer you've achieved full understanding.

- Help your customer realize he or she learned more about his or her needs through conversation with you.

- Determine if you know enough to make a proper recommendation.

- Show your customer you know enough to make a good recommendation.

- Prove to yourself you've achieved a relationship where the customer will value and trust your recommendation.

- Create an anticipation or looking forward to what you will recommend.

and

- Take your customer in an organized fashion through the lows of his or her Reality Trough, finishing on the emotional high associated with hope and a deeper expectation that he or she can gain the desired extra benefits.

Failing to show full understanding creates objections. The customer sees the flaws in any recommendation that comes from a failure to understand his or her needs.

THE PROCESS TO SHOW FULL UNDERSTANDING

Summarize in a brief and organized fashion to help your customer organize his or her own understanding.

The Process To Show Understanding

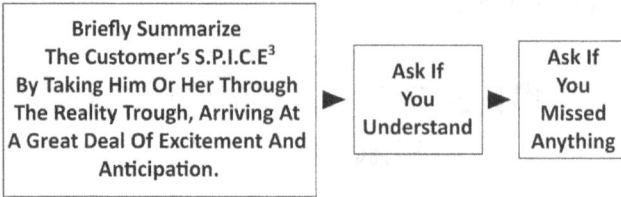

Briefly Summarize The Customer's S.P.I.C.E³ By Taking Him Or Her Through The Reality Trough, Arriving At A Great Deal Of Excitement And Anticipation.	▶	Ask If You Understand	▶	Ask If You Missed Anything

Organize your summary in terms of the information that is the customer's S.P.I.C.E³ and take him or her through the Reality Trough. This summary should induce the range of feelings from the low point of the Reality Trough to the excitement and anticipation of his or her desired E³ outcomes.

1. Make a brief reference to what you learned about your customer's current situation.

2. Remind your customer about key symptoms and real problems.

3. Then summarize what those problems cost – both tangible and intangible costs. (*Induce all of the emotions associated with this expanded awareness of the costs.*)

4. Describe the real constraints that must be resolved with your solution. (*Stimulate the emotions of frustration and disappointment associated with being stuck.*)

5. Cover any underlying expectations about what the new solution must minimally accomplish.

6. Enthusiastically summarize the exciting benefits or results the customer now expects to gain by any solution you will recommend. (*Induce the emotions of excitement and anticipation.*)

7. Ask if your customer is ready to hear what you intend to recommend.

Periodically ask if you've understood everything to keep the customer involved and set up a "yes" framework. Look for any clues indicating you've misunderstood or missed something. If so, back up, ask more questions and use the active listening skills to learn what you need to know.

When To Move To The Next Step

Move to the next step when:

- the customer indicates you have full understanding,
- the customer is showing positive non-verbal clues and an eagerness to hear your recommendation,
- the customer is showing a readiness to buy, and
- you have the product knowledge necessary to make the right recommendation.

Either move to Half Time or to the step where you present your recommendation.

Transition To Half Time

Tell the customer you'll find the best solution for his or her needs and get back when you're ready to make your recommendation.

"George, I'm excited about getting you the best possible solution. I need a few minutes to get it organized. While I'm gone, please complete this leasing application to allow us to proceed as soon as possible. As we learned in the discussion of your needs, there would be real value in spreading out the payment. There's no reason to delay when you can realize greater value right away. I'll only be a few minutes."

Transition To Make Your Recommendation

On the other hand, if you took your Half Time break after learning the customer's S.P.I.C.E^3, then returned to the customer and completed an effective summary of his or her S.P.I.C.E^3, then move to Step Five and Make Your Recommendation. The customer is eager to hear it.

"Jacob, I'm confident I can solve your problems, get you benefits you don't get now, and reduce your costs. Are you ready to hear what I propose?"

THE SECOND HALF OF THE SALES PROCESS

Now, you're going to provide a complete solution to satisfy the customer's expectations, excitements, and eagerness, while further enhancing your relationship with your client. You're also going to get this sale.

Step Five – Make Your Recommendation

> *Present your complete solution and fulfill all of your customer's needs (his or her S.P.I.C.E^3) – nothing less.*

It's time for you to achieve the sale. It's time for the customer to get his or her benefits. Give your customer the recommendation he or she is eagerly anticipating.

GOALS OF STEP FIVE – MAKE YOUR RECOMMENDATION

- Recommend what you think is the best solution for your customer (*to help your customer achieve greater success*).
- Suggest a complete solution.
- Make one recommendation, not many, as it confuses the customer (*only offer the one right solution*).
- Match your recommendation to the benefits your customer wants to buy.
- Convey your enthusiasm for your recommended solution.

and

- Get it so right the only decision can be "Yes".

THE RECOMMENDATION PROCESS

1. Tell the customer this solution will yield the benefits of (*re-state what the customer previously told you he or she expects and wants.*)

2. With enthusiasm, specify the complete solution that would best fit your customer's needs. Do not get caught up in product detail. Stay focused on the complete set of products and services as the correct solution.

3. Give your customer the total price and compare this price to the costs of his or her status quo.

4. Tell your customer again how this solution gives him or her the exciting benefits and relieves the costs or the pain of the status quo.

5. Lastly, invite and answer questions in a manner that educates your customer so he or she can make an informed decision.

"Mr. Crofton, this solution assures you and your customers that all of your deliveries within this 25 mile radius will arrive at the correct destination within one hour, reducing lost sales, and increasing your ability to fulfill customer orders, hours and even days faster than your competitors. This will keep your customers' inventory costs down. We're confident this will make you a preferred supplier. We can guarantee 100% performance on this promise because, based on your volume, we'll have a fleet of trucks exclusively devoted to your business. They'll even sport your logo. It will be like you have your own fleet, but without the concerns of hiring drivers, maintaining the vehicles, and acquiring complete insurance coverage. This will save you money, and increase your profits by 15% based on our calculations for the volume you had in the last six months. That's important, correct?"

Do Not Talk Product – Talk Complete Solution

Do not talk about individual products and features at this stage. Talk about everything together as a solution. If the customer asks a question about a specific product, then answer that question. You only need to talk about those aspects of the product the customer asks you to talk about.

Stay focused on the complete solution and the benefits that matter to this particular customer. Speak in a language your client understands.

Involve Your Customer

Check with your customer throughout your presentation about his or her understanding of your recommendation. As you mention a benefit, ask if the customer agrees the benefit is important. If you lose the customer's attention, understanding, enthusiasm, or trust, stop your presentation. Ask what your customer thinks so far and shift into using the active listening skills.

Present The Complete Solution

Present the total suggested package of goods and services. No surprises. Don't recommend the primary item, get the customer's decision to buy, and then spring another recommendation to buy a bunch of add-ons.

TALK TOTAL PRICE AND TOTAL VALUE

Tell the customer the total price and specify any payment amounts. Outline the payment schedule. Compare the total price to the costs of the status quo, the desired benefits, and the anticipated financial gains he or she can expect to achieve.

ANSWER YOUR CUSTOMER'S QUESTIONS

Answer any questions or concerns (*and only those questions or concerns*) that your customer has about about your recommendation. Paraphrase the question to be sure you understand what the customer wants to know.

A COMPLETE SOLUTION

A complete solution should contain:

* specific goods or primary services plus all accessories,

* related services such as delivery, installation, maintenance, integration with other goods already in place, training, disposal of old unwanted goods, investment protection plans, subsequent end of life disposal for the new products,

* supplies, and

* finance arrangements.

If unable to deliver a complete solution that truly meets the customer's needs at this time, then make this clear to the customer in an open declaration.

REQUISITE SKILLS

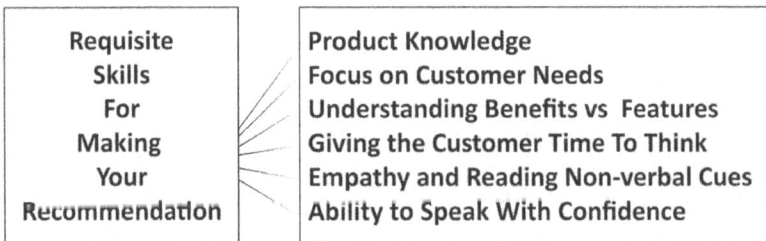

Requisite Skills For Making Your Recommendation	Product Knowledge Focus on Customer Needs Understanding Benefits vs Features Giving the Customer Time To Think Empathy and Reading Non-verbal Cues Ability to Speak With Confidence

- Have enough product knowledge to make the proper recommendation. Use Half Time to get the product knowledge you need.

- Think about the products and services only in terms of the client's needs. What matters is what the products and services will do for the client.

- Describe or show your recommendation, state the benefits, and then be quiet as the customer thinks about what you've proposed.

- Maintain your empathy at this stage. Read your client's non-verbal cues and look for behaviours that suggest disagreement, uneasiness, or confusion. Suspend your selling efforts if you detect any client resistance or objection.

- Present enthusiastically so your customer can feel enthusiastic about owning the solution.

- Everything comprising the solution should be presented as a complete solution that provides the benefits the customer wants to achieve.

- Avoid using jargon as you present your solution. Speak clearly about the benefits in plain language.

- Present your recommendations with confidence and enthusiasm.

- Make your recommendations concisely and with style. Say enough to explain why the solution you're recommending meets the customer's needs, then shut up and let the customer digest the information.

MUST BE THE RIGHT SOLUTION

If the solution is not fully capable of yielding the benefits the customer now expects, you shouldn't be recommending it. If there are any limitations to your solution that mean you can not provide all of the benefits the customer has come to expect, you must be completely clear with your customer about those limitations.

BREAK OLD HABITS

If you've been spending a lot of time talking about products or services and their features, you need to force yourself to shift your focus. Comment on the whole solution as opposed to its parts and components.

WHEN TO MOVE TO ASKING FOR A DECISION

Move to asking for the business when:

- You've uncovered all of the relevant information about the client's needs.

- The right solution for those needs has been identified.

- You've presented your complete recommendation with enthusiasm and a clear demonstration of how benefits exceed price.

- Buying cues are evident, such as the customer nodding his or her head in agreement throughout the presentation of your recommendation.

and

- All of the client's responses to your presentation ratify that you've matched the benefits of the solution to his or her needs.

If you aren't here yet, and see hesitation on the part of the customer, back up and clarify any reservations the customer might hold.

TRANSITION TO THE ACTION STEP

Move to Step Six by declaring you believe your recommendation meets your customer's needs and provides real value resulting in extra benefits compared to his or her current situation. If your client appears to share your excitement, then move to the next step and lead the customer to his or her decision.

"I'm pleased this solution meets your needs, reduces your costs, and gives you added value by (*producing desired benefit*). Do you agree? Do you share my excitement?"

Step Six – Ask How To Proceed

(Invite The Customer To Make A Purchase Decision)

> *You don't need a tool chest full of manipulative closes. You just ask the customer what he or she would like to do next.*

Once you've presented your recommendation to your customer, the next step is the action step. You initiate a call-to-action because it's time for the customer to decide.

Goals Of Step Six – Ask How To Proceed

- Move the customer to take the next appropriate action.

- Make it clear what is going to happen next so you both know what to expect.

- Initiate the purchase in a way that is comfortable for the customer, and fits with the information the client has given you about him or herself.

- Deal constructively with any customer questions, concerns or objections.

and

- Win the customer's business in such a way he or she will make referrals to others because he or she knows you can be trusted to look after friends, family members, and colleagues just like you've taken care of the customer.

Time For The Customer To Decide

Invite the customer to simply make a decision. You have an ethical responsibility to get the customer to choose an optimum solution that delivers the results he or she wants.

Asking for the business could trigger the following concerns:

- Do I really need this product?

- Will buying this product really make a positive difference?

- Does this product measure up to what the competition has available?

- Should I postpone buying?

- Will this supplier stand behind the product?

- What will my friends/peers think if I buy this item?

- Is this person trying to get me to buy the right solution?

However, if you've matched your presentation to the needs of the client and have presented the complete solution clearly indicating the benefits the customer will realize, all of these concerns will have been dealt with.

When To Ask

If you and the customer fully understand your client's needs, if you've summarized to demonstrate full understanding, if you've made a recommendation matched to those needs and desired benefits, if you've explained the benefits with enthusiasm, and if you've attended to the client's responses to your information and detected a positive response, initiate a call-to-action.

Recognize Buying Signals

Positive signals the retail customer is ready to buy include behaviours such as:

- a positive head nod,

- the customer reaching for a credit card, cheque book or wallet,

- a wife looking at her husband, making eye contact and nodding,

- a question about availability or delivery, or

- when the customer says something indicating he or she is ready to buy what you've recommended, such as, "Okay", or "I'll take it", or "I think I'll also take some XXXXXX with that".

The customer is essentially saying, "I want this", so take him or her to the till.

Positive signals the corporate customer is ready to buy include behaviours such as:

- managers looking at each other and nodding in affirmation,

- smiles as people read your proposal or listen to your presentation,

- use of a calculator at the meeting table,
- reviewing calendars to judge time lines for implementation,
- asking for testimonials from other clients,
- asking for your corporate financials to validate the stability of your company,
- questions about implementation or asking to meet with your specialists to discuss installation, or
- comments like, "We'll need to get a purchase order for this." or "Okay, let's go meet with Purchasing."

When you see a buying signal, try a call-to-action. It's your responsibility to either:

- move forward to the next stage in the customer's decision-making process and get the sale, or
- back up to gather more information if your customer isn't satisfied your recommendation meets his or her needs, or
- get feedback from the customer as to why you didn't earn his or her business.

HOW TO ASK FOR A DECISION

You've managed to get the customer to the place where he or she can make an informed decision to purchase a complete solution. Now it's up to your customer to decide.

OPTION 1 – ASK DIRECTLY

If you're fairly confident you've built sufficient rapport, and you see positive responses to your recommendation on the part of the client, ask directly.

"George, this solution excites me. Shall we go ahead?"

OPTION 2 – DECLARE AND ASK

Indicate you want to win the customer's business and then ask for the sale.

"Samantha. I'm glad that this solution was available because it gives you all of the benefits we discussed. I want to win your business. Have I done so?

OPTION 3 – ASSUME THE BUSINESS

If you believe the customer is absolutely ready to buy, just initiate the transaction.

"Should I set up the appointment for delivery tomorrow?"

OPTION 4 – WHEN UNCERTAIN OF CUSTOMER READINESS

If you aren't quite sure the customer is ready, ask for the business by saying something like,

"This solution is right for you. What do you want to do now?"

or

"Have I met your needs?"

or

"How would you like to proceed from here?"

Just ask straight up. It would be dangerous to keep talking. It's time to stop, ask and listen.

CALL-TO-ACTION OUTCOMES

The customer could:

- make a decision to buy,

- make a commitment to make a decision to buy by a set time frame,

- make a commitment to discuss the solution with significant others who are involved in making the decision to buy,

- ask questions or raise concerns, or

- make a declaration he or she is going to do something else (*such as check out what one of your competitors has to offer*).

If the customer's response is a decision to buy, then complete the transaction and shift to the next step.

IF THE CUSTOMER HASN'T YET DECIDED TO BUY

If you detect any reservation on the part of the customer, stop and check.

"I sense a hesitation on your part and I'm wondering if I've failed to take into consideration one of your needs. As your consultant, I want to help you get the complete solution to the problems we discussed, and get it implemented so you experience the benefits sooner than later. So if I haven't done my job, please let me know what concerns you."

IF THE CUSTOMER WANTS TO DELAY

Simply summarize the benefits you understand the customer is looking for and set a specific date and time when you will call.

"Mrs. Cressman, we've discussed the problems you're trying to solve, the costs of those problems, and the benefits you're hoping to achieve. It's important that you get a solution that allows you to (*summarize the E^3 Benefits*). I really want you to realize the gains a proper solution can give you, and will follow-up with you. I think we both recognize the sooner you begin to experience the benefits, the better it will be. The solution I've proposed will get you going right away. When can I call you to follow-up?"

IF THE CUSTOMER WANTS TO DISCUSS WITH SIGNIFICANT OTHERS

Alternatively, if your customer just needs to discuss his or her decision-making with someone else, then give room to do so.

"This is a significant investment and I understand the need to discuss this with your spouse. If there's any information you need from me to help you do so, let me know. Given the significance of the benefits you would realize by making this change, when can I contact you to follow-up? Is Tuesday okay?"

IF THE CUSTOMER WANTS TO CHECK THE COMPETITION

If the customer intends to shop around or check with your competition, acknowledge the importance of this decision. Offer to help the customer review any new information he or she might be given. Never say anything disparaging about the competition.

> "Jim. It's a large investment and you want to know you're making the correct decision. I can appreciate the wish to shop around. Make sure the people you talk with take the time to discuss your needs. They should get to know your particular expectations and desired outcomes. Check out pricing but the real issue is getting all of the results we discussed today by putting a complete solution in place. The solution you buy should give you (*the E^3 Benefits*). I'll call you tomorrow at 10:00 a.m. to see how your visit to our competitors turned out for you. If you get new information that appears to conflict with what I told you, I'll help you sort out the differences."

IF THE CUSTOMER RESISTS A FOLLOW-UP CALL

If there is any resistance to scheduling a follow-up call, ask for feedback. You've given a significant amount of time to this customer with a pure intention of being an effective insight-oriented consultant. If you failed to achieve a sale, the least you want to accomplish is a learning experience.

Ask the customer for his or her impressions of you and what you've done in this conversation. For example,

> "Frank, it was my intention today to get to know your full set of needs so I could make a proper recommendation, one that would give you the benefits you deserve. It would appear I didn't do my job as effectively as I could have, and I've somehow disappointed you. I want to learn to be a more effective consultant and would like your feedback as to how I failed you today."

Dealing With Questions, Concerns and Objections

A question is a request for more information so the customer can decide whether or not to buy. A concern is an expression of worry about one or more aspects of your recommendation. An objection, like a concern, is an expression of a problem or a reason the customer isn't yet ready. An objection usually has more intensity than a concern.

However, questions, concerns and objections are all indications the customer does want to buy from you. Otherwise the customer could just end your meeting and buy elsewhere.

Dealing With Questions

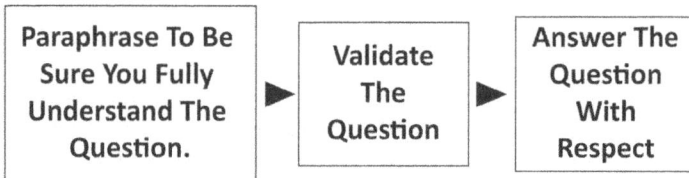

A question, no matter how expressed, is a request for information and the best way to deal with it is to understand the question and then provide the needed information.

Dealing With Questions

Paraphrase To Be Sure You Fully Understand The Question.	▶	Validate The Question	▶	Answer The Question With Respect

First paraphrase the question before you answer it. Make sure you understand the question, validate its importance, and then answer it. Answer questions informatively and with care. Avoid offering more information than what the customer has asked for as this can just add confusion.

S: "It sounds like you're asking me if I think there is something better about this brand than the one sold by our competitor, or if I think the other brand is inferior in some way, is that correct?"

C: "Yes, is there something better about this brand that I should know?"

S: "That's a good question. Actually, both are good brands. I recommended the one I did because this particular model has all of the features you need to achieve the benefits you value the most. You want to be able to (*desired result*) and this XXXXXX will do that very well."

DEALING WITH CONCERNS

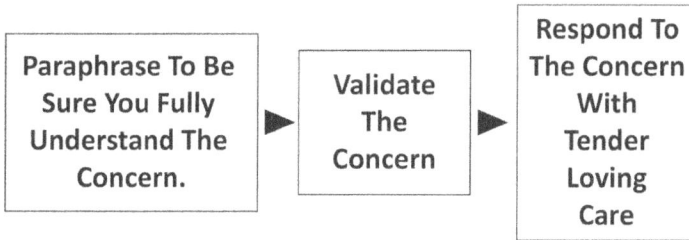

The customer may disclose a reservation about buying what you recommended because he or she is not yet confident it will meet his or her needs.

Dealing With Concerns

Paraphrase To Be Sure You Fully Understand The Concern.	▶	Validate The Concern	▶	Respond To The Concern With Tender Loving Care

Paraphrase the concern first. Summarize what you think the customer means then ask if you've understood his or her concern. Once you know you understand, validate the concern. Agree with the concern as an important issue or consideration. Make sure you keep an open mind then address the concern with tender loving care. Give your opinion constructively and not argumentatively. If the concern isn't addressed by your recommendation, change your recommendation.

C: (*with exasperated voice*) "Boy I sure would hate to buy this today and then find out it went on sale right away. I wouldn't want to discover that if I waited, I would have gotten a better price."

S: (***Paraphrase***) "So Jeff, I sense you're concerned about whether or not we're giving you a good enough deal today."

C: "Yeah, I wouldn't want to buy because you're such a great sales guy, and miss out on a better deal."

91

S: (**Validate**) "I understand. We share the concern as well. We don't want you to pay more than you have to. (**Answer**) Actually, we do a lot to make sure you get the best price. We're part of a national chain and as such we get the advantage of large volume buying. That's part of the savings we bring to you. We shop our competition every day to check their prices against ours. In addition, we have a price guarantee. If you find a lower price on any of these items within the next thirty days, come back to us, and we'll refund you the difference.

C: "Sounds good."

S: "However, remember if you don't put this solution into effect as soon as possible, you do have costs right now. We talked about your current situation – how you aren't able to get some of your work done within your deadlines, how you're spending long hours of personal time just trying to keep up. This will get you working faster and spending your time more effectively. There's a lot of benefit here exceeding the price of your investment in this solution. We protect you on price so you can get this today, and make the necessary changes in how you do your work."

C: "You're right. Let's proceed."

DEALING WITH OBJECTIONS

First, prevent objections by:

- building an open relationship where the customer tells you his or her full story,

- listening for full understanding,

- facilitating new insights about the customer's situation, problems, costs, constraints and expectations to the point the customer reaches an excitement about what could be achieved,

- uncovering the customer's needs so you both know there is a reason to buy,

- checking your understanding with a summary checkout, and

- recommending the right solution, a complete solution providing the benefits the customer wants to buy.

However, if you do get an objection, or what appears to be an objection, discover what's behind the customer's concern. Be calm. Be the most resistant person to the sale. You only want to sell what's right for the customer. So find out what's right.

Dealing With Objections

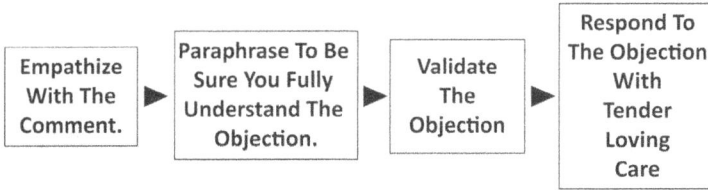

Empathize With The Comment.	▶	Paraphrase To Be Sure You Fully Understand The Objection.	▶	Validate The Objection	▶	Respond To The Objection With Tender Loving Care

Don't get anxious and uptight. Just deal with the objection as an indication to back up and get more information. Return to the needs assessment stage and learn what you didn't learn then.

1. First **empathize** with the comment. "I sense a major concern regarding what I recommended, and your concern is important to me."

2. Secondly, **paraphrase** to see if there is an underlying meaning to address. Perhaps, the objection is different than it might first appear. "Sounds like you think this XXXXXX isn't fast enough for your needs, correct?"

3. Thirdly, **validate** the objection you uncover as you paraphrase for understanding. "I agree with your concern. It's important and should be addressed."

4. Lastly, **respond** to the concern or objection. This might mean either changing your recommendation, or just explaining it differently so the customer is more comfortable. *(It should not mean reducing your price. If your solution has real value where benefits exceed price, then price is not the issue.)*

The process may surface new information, which means the recommendation should be changed. Understand it, validate it and then use it to change your recommendation. You want to recommend the right solution – not push what you originally recommended. The most resistant person to the sale of a wrong product and service – one that does not meet the customer's needs – should be you.

C: "I just don't think this is right for me. It doesn't meet any of our company standards in terms of brand, and the required configuration. They're pretty sticky about that stuff."

S: (**Empathize**) "Sounds like I missed a key piece. (**Paraphrase**) Your company has specific brand requirements and only supports systems with specific features. Is this correct?

C: "Yeah. I didn't bring it up earlier because I forgot it was an important consideration. I didn't realize until I saw what you're recommending, and this isn't a brand they would support. Without their support, I'm kind of useless. I don't know enough about this stuff."

S: (**Validate**) "That's pretty significant. It's important we follow your company's preferences. (**Answer By Learning More**) It seems to me I need to know more about this. Can you explain the requirements to me?"

THINGS NOT TO DO

- Don't argue with your customer. Don't put yourself in an adversarial and intractable position.

- Don't ignore the objection.

- Don't use the "what if" approach to deflect the objection.

- Don't just give up on the customer and leave.

- Don't plead with the customer.

- Don't capitulate and break company rules to satisfy the customer and get the sale.

- Don't criticize the competition.

- Don't minimize the significance of the customer's objection.

- Don't belittle the customer's concern in any way.

- Don't make exaggerated and generalized claims about what your solution can do.

- Don't criticize competitive brands.

- Don't try to persuade the customer away from his or her concern by appealing to his or her ego.

WHEN TO MOVE TO THE NEXT STEP

Your call-to-action question should take the two of you to one of four possibilities acceptable to you as the salesperson. The customer could:

- decide to buy,

- ask a question or express a concern or objection,

- negotiate a specific time frame within which you will call to follow-up (*to help the customer with his or her decision making, or to discuss the actual decision*), or

- give you feedback about how you failed to earn his or her business.

Your call-to-action should not end up with a "wishy-washy" outcome where the customer promises to get back to you because he or she is going away to think about it, and quite possibly shop around.

When you see a non-verbal signal or hear a direct statement indicating the customer has decided to buy your recommended solution, move to the next step. If the customer declares that he or she isn't going to buy at this time, transition to the next step. Negotiate a specific day and time to call in order to review the customer's decision, or to help the customer with his or her decision-making process.

TRANSITION TO REINFORCE THE CUSTOMER'S DECISION

Make a brief comment acknowledging that a decision has been made, and then launch into Step Seven to reinforce the validity of that decision.

"Bill, that's great. I'm glad you've made your decision."

Step Seven – Reinforce The Decision

Let your customer know he or she has made the right choice. Show respect for your customer's decision by affirming it.

Regardless of which outcome you've achieved, fortify the decision with a positive comment saying your customer has done the right thing. This is a very short and simple step.

GOALS OF REINFORCING THE CUSTOMER'S DECISION

- Cement your customer's understanding that what you've recommended really does meet his or her needs, priorities, and buying criteria.

- Give your customer the words to say if anyone else challenges or questions his or her decision.

- Remind your customer of your commitment to make sure he or she gets the best possible solution.

- Demonstrate your respect for your customer and the decisions he or she makes.

- Sustain the glue in the relationship you've been building with this client.

and

- Show your customer he or she can feel good about the decision.

IF YOUR CUSTOMER HAS DECIDED TO BUY FROM YOU

1. Declare the correctness of your customer's decision.

2. Express envy or say something about how others will think your customer made a great choice.

3. Remind your customer about the benefits and value he or she will realize.

4. Congratulate your customer.

5. Transition to the next step of thanking your customer and arranging follow-up.

   "Bill, I agree with your choice. You wanted a solution that does __X___ , ___Y___ , and ___Z___ . This will do that for you. I think it's the perfect choice and I'm pretty excited about the results you'll get. The benefits will far exceed your investment. Your boss will be very impressed."

IF THE CUSTOMER HAS DECIDED TO BUY ELSEWHERE

1. Declare the correctness of your customer's decision to buy a new solution now.

2. Remind your customer about the benefits and value that should be realized from this solution.

3. Congratulate the customer on making a decision and taking action.

4. Indicate your desire to earn your customer's business and even your disappointment that you did not.

5. Ask for and get feedback about your own performance.

6. Transition to the next step of thanking the customer and arranging follow-up.

"George, I'm glad you found a solution to your needs. It was clear to both of us you could reduce your current costs by getting a new XXXXXX, and the right package would get you benefits which would more than pay for the purchase. Specifically, this new solution should (*list the specific benefits your customer wants to realize*). I congratulate you for taking action. Of course, I'm disappointed we failed to earn your business, but I value our relationship and I believe getting a solution now was the smart choice. However, I would appreciate getting your feedback as to how I failed to earn your business this time. Do you have a few minutes to tell me?"

IF YOUR CUSTOMER HAS DECIDED NOT TO BUY AT THIS TIME

1. If the proper solution to the customer's S.P.I.C.E[3] is not yet available, convince the customer to wait for the right solution.

2. If your competitor has what your customer needs and you don't, then make a referral to your competitor so your customer achieves success.

3. If your customer decides to postpone buying a solution now, reinforce the customer's decision, while also encouraging your customer to actively measure the current costs of the problem(s) and to think about whether the constraints are real impediments to taking action now.

4. Tell your customer you will follow up periodically to make sure he or she is still okay with this decision. Make a note in your day timer for when you should be calling the customer back.

"Sam, I think your decision is the correct one for you at this time. The solution I'm recommending today doesn't appear to have enough value in your mind to justify making the investment. I think you would be wise to spend more time assessing the problems you have, measuring how much they really cost, and examining the constraints keeping you from making a change today. I believe what I recommended is the right solution, but agree you should postpone until you believe this yourself. So measure your costs now. Then we can determine if the return on your investment will be high enough for you to feel okay deciding to put this solution in place."

REINFORCING THE CUSTOMER'S DECISION WON'T WORK IF:

- You haven't really learned your customer's full S.P.I.C.E^3, and have no way to show him or her what the solution will actually do.

- You've persuaded your customer to buy despite his or her initial resistance.

- You've sold your customer up to a price point he or she can't really justify by the limited benefits the products will yield.

- You've totally ignored the recommendations your customer received from his or her influencers, and made a different recommendation of your own without a clear demonstration of the added benefits.

or,

- You've acted less than enthusiastically when you expressed your reinforcement.

WHEN TO MOVE TO THE NEXT STEP

Move to the next step when you've said your reinforcing remarks. Having reinforced the customer's decision, no matter what it is, your relationship should still be intact. If not, then back up and make repairs. Trust the work you did as you followed the "GET SMARTER" sales approach.

TRANSITION TO THE THANK YOU AND FOLLOW-UP

If your customer bought from you,

> "Bill, I envy you for what you just bought. You've got the coolest XXXXXX. I wish I had one myself. I also want to thank you."

If the customer bought from your competitor,

> "Ron, I'm glad you found a solution to solve your problem even though it is disappointing to lose out this time. It's great you'll be able to reduce your costs of maintenance, produce a wider variety of products for your customers, and will realize those better profits we talked about. I'd like to take a moment to say thanks."

If the customer put off buying at this time,

> "Frank, I'm glad we had a chance to talk, and agree it's wise to wait for now. I'll keep my eyes open for the best solution for your needs. I'd like to thank you for giving me this opportunity."

Be sincere when making these comments. Enhance the relationship by showing respect. Let the customer know you think he or she has made the best decision for his or her needs.

STEP EIGHT – THANK YOU AND FOLLOW-UP

The sale, or even a lost sale, is only the beginning. You have a relationship to manage for the lifetime of your customer. Show appreciation to your customer for the opportunity to earn his or her business. Stay in touch.

Offer a thank-you and make an arrangement to follow-up with the customer after he or she has had time to put the solution into practice.

THE GOALS OF STEP EIGHT

- Contact the customer to inquire about any problems before he or she calls you (*or before your competitor calls if the customer bought elsewhere*).

- Solidify the long-term relationship you started with this first transaction.

- Be defined by your customer as his or her "go to" expert, the person the customer will turn to in all future situations where he or she needs the products and services you sell.

- Maintain ongoing contact with this customer who will buy again and again, and refer family and friends.

- Become your customer's advocate in any future dealings with your organization.

and

- Show you value him or her as a "customer for life".

'THANK YOU AND FOLLOW-UP' EVERY TIME

Show gratitude. We're in a very competitive world. Make sure your customer knows you value his or her business no matter how large (*or small*) the sale. The sale does not end once the customer has decided to buy. If you did the relationship building properly while doing Steps One to Seven, you're now in a long-term relationship. Think of this customer as your "customer for life".

Never lose a sale without very sincerely thanking the customer for giving you the chance to earn his or her business. If the customer bought from a competitor, show just as much gratitude as if he or she bought from you. You can share your disappointment over losing the sale but you should still express appreciation that the customer gave his or her time to engage in a conversation with you.

Always give your customer instructions as to how to reach you. Give him or her a business card. Tell your customer how to reach you by giving your telephone numbers, your work hours, and the name of your back-up person when you aren't around.

Remind your customer you will be contacting him or her to follow-up in order to check that everything functions correctly. Inspect to make sure your customer is experiencing the benefits you promised.

SAYING "THANK YOU"

1. Remember it's the right thing to do, whether you get a sale or not.

and,

2. Do it in such a way that your "thank you" stands out as sincere.

"Thank you for coming in today. I really appreciate this opportunity to earn your business."

or

"I'm very grateful that we had this chance to talk. Our conversation has been very interesting to me and I hope rewarding for you."

THE TIMES TO SAY "THANKS"

1. The first happens when you say, "Thank You" just after you've reinforced your customer's decision.

2. The second happens while you help your customer through the transaction.

3. The third happens immediately after the transaction as you assist your customer to get the goods into his or her possession, and any services implemented.

4. The fourth happens in follow-up after the customer has installed and is using the new solution.

5. The fifth occurs when your customer turns to you again in the future to buy something else, or you make another visit as a corporate salesperson.

AFTER REINFORCING

Right after reinforcing your customer's decision, show that you value your customer's choice to give you his or her business or to give you a chance to earn that business. Your message of appreciation should follow so closely after giving your reinforcing remarks it seems to be part of that step.

> "Sandy, by implementing this solution you just reduced your monthly costs by $3,000, added the ability to do (*what the customer was excited about doing*) and made the job much more pleasurable for your people. I sure want to thank you for letting me help you add to your success."

or

> "Joan, I really appreciate your coming in today and giving us your business. I really enjoyed our talk and I feel good about what you'll gain when you use this XXXXXX."

DURING THE TRANSACTION

Make the transaction easier and faster by ensuring proper invoicing or transaction processes are followed. Help out at the till, or watch the process of preparing the solution for shipping and make sure the invoice is prepared the way the customer has been led to believe it would be. Make sure the goods and services are provided on time and as promised.

> "Mr. Grantham, I really appreciate your meeting with me today, and spending time with me as we explored your needs. I'm glad we found a great solution for you that will (*summary of the benefits you just sold*). I expect that your family will be very impressed. Thank you again."

IMMEDIATELY AFTER THE TRANSACTION

Before your customer leaves the store, or before you leave the customer's premises, say, "Thank You" so the customer knows you truly appreciate the opportunity to earn his or her business. Then arrange to make a follow-up call so you can check to make sure everything is working as expected.

"(*while shaking her hand*) Sally, thank you once again for your business. You've made a great choice and it's really going to pay off. I expect to hear a lot of excitement in your voice when I call in two days to find out how this is working out for you. However, in the event you have any concerns or questions before I call, please call me at (###) ###-#### extension ###. If you don't get me, leave a message or contact Bill at extension ###. He's my back-up and will make sure we take care of you."

MAINTAIN FOLLOW-UP CONTACT WITH YOUR CUSTOMERS

- Complete a scheduled follow-up call within three days of the solution being implemented at your customer's site.

- Call as scheduled to follow-up any quote you gave to your customer.

- Remember the customer's name and use it often when he or she visits your location, or calls you, or meets you in any subsequent meetings.

- Make sure you call the customer to establish if any problems have arisen before he or she calls you.

- Send the customer special notes – "thank you" notes after his or her purchase; new information you know meets your customer's needs; personalized marketing letters and updates on the products and services your firm sells; preferably in material which illustrates how these products and services might solve your customer's unique problems.

FOLLOW-UP CALLS

Differentiate yourself and your organization by calling your customer within three days of having dealt with him or her. Call after your customer has made a major purchase and advise him or her you're checking to make sure everything is okay.

Enter into such a call with an open mind. Expect three possible outcomes:

- The customer might be quite satisfied.

- The customer might have realized he or she needs something in addition.

- The customer might be having a problem with the implementation of his or her new purchase.

Do not expect the worst. Do not expect a perfectly happy customer. Just call to find out how the customer is doing.

A HAPPY CUSTOMER

Show your customer you remember his or her reasons for buying by asking if the solution meets those specific needs. Ask if your customer is pleased with the results he or she gets when using your solution.

> "Jacob, good morning. This is Sandra from Qualico. I'm calling as I said I would to see if your new equipment works the way it should. Did you speed up your production, and did this new technology give you the ability to do new work you couldn't do before? Is everything going according to our plan?"

A CUSTOMER WHO NEEDS SOMETHING NEW

Don't ask if the customer needs anything else. However, if a new need exists at this time, your customer will likely volunteer his or her need. If you find you've called a customer who needs something new, remember to get his or her new S.P.I.C.E[3] and use the insight-oriented consultative process in this new opportunity.

A CUSTOMER WITH A PROBLEM

If you call a customer who has a problem with the solution you provided, impress the customer by getting the problem resolved. Become your customer's advocate. Get your organization to take care of your customer properly.

> "Sue, I regret that this has happened and I want to get it fixed right away. I'll talk to our service people and get this addressed quickly. Is that okay with you?"

If the customer bought elsewhere and is encountering a problem, provide information that facilitates resolution of the problem. Give suggestions as to how the customer can induce the organization that got the sale to properly fix the issue.

THE FOLLOW-UP TELEPHONE CALL

An effective follow-up telephone call should:

- be made within three days of the customer's purchase,

- be made at a reasonable hour or time of day,

- be made when your customer expects your call because you told him or her you would call,

- be opened with an enthusiastic greeting,

- be supported by a clear and positive reason reminding the customer why you're calling,

- contain a reference to the benefits the customer expected to get prior to making the purchase, and

- include a check to see if everything is working properly and the customer is realizing those benefits.

For example:

[**Enthusiastic Greeting**] "Hello Bill, this is Doug, your consultant at Hudsonia Computers."

[**Reason For Call**] "As we discussed when you made your purchase the other day, I'm calling to see how the solution is working for you."

[**Expected Benefits**] "When we talked about your needs the other day, you mentioned you wanted to use the computer to engage in day trading over the Internet to maximize your return on your investments.

[**Check For Satisfaction**] Are you able to do what you wanted with this equipment? Is everything operating properly and meeting the needs we discussed?"

Paraphrase and summarize whatever the customer tells you about his or her experience with the new purchase. If your customer indicates there are problems, make sure you achieve full understanding then respond appropriately to what you learn. If a problem has been identified, offer the solution.

On the other hand, if your customer makes a positive comment, convey your understanding that everything is working satisfactorily and once again, reinforce your customer's decision. Close with a thank you and an invitation to call if he or she needs anything. If the call has been very positive in nature, you have the option to close the call with an invitation to refer friends and colleagues.

> "Bill, it's my job to look after my customers. I want to make sure you're happy with my work, and with (*name of your organization*). If you have any friends or colleagues you would like to receive the same care and attention, please don't hesitate to call me, or get them to call me themselves. I promise you I'll take good care of them as well."

FOLLOW-UP CALLS AFTER GIVING A WRITTEN QUOTE

When you give a quote, tell the customer you'll be calling to see how his or her decision-making is going and to see how to be of further help. Arrange the call then make it.

An effective follow-up call after giving the customer a quote should:

- be made within three days of having given the quote,

- have been pre-arranged with the customer,

- be opened with an enthusiastic greeting, and

- clearly state the reason for the call.

For example,

> S: "Hello Mr. Hook, this is Bill Smith, your consultant at (*name of your company*)."

> C: "Oh hi Bill."

> S: "As we discussed the other day, I'm calling to see how things are going in your efforts to find a suitable solution to your

needs. Have you made your decision yet, or is there anything I can do to help you?"

There are several possible things you could discover:

- The customer could be undecided, confused and trying to sort through the information.

- The customer could be right on the edge of making a decision to buy from you.

- The customer could be right on the edge of making a decision to buy from a competitor.

- The customer might have already purchased from a competitor.

- The customer could be trying to "ditch you" because he or she is unhappy with you.

CALLING THE UNDECIDED CUSTOMER

- Offer your help to sort through the information so he or she can make an informed decision.

- Provide the information the customer needs to overcome his or her confusion.

- Check to see if the customer has realized something new about his or her needs.

or

- Answer the customer's questions.

If the customer is undecided and confused, find an opening in the conversation and say something like,

"George, I agree – it can be very confusing figuring out which XXXXXX is best for your needs. As a consultant, it's my goal to help my clients make the best possible decision. Do you have any questions I can answer for you?"

Paraphrase any questions to be sure you understand what really confuses your customer, or leaves him or her hesitant to act, and then answer the questions. Once the customer is no longer confused, initiate a call-to-action.

Calling The Customer Who Is About To Purchase Elsewhere

You would still indicate you are calling to help your customer to make a decision by answering any questions. If the customer hesitates, or anything suggests he or she isn't comfortable, do a feelings check. Maintain the attitude reflected in the statement, "I really want this customer to be successful."

Your conversation might lead to further helping the customer make his or her decision. You could answer questions about a recommendation received from the competitor. Answer the questions truthfully and without disparaging the competition in any way. Or you may simply learn you lost the sale and the reasons why. If so, you will learn information about your competition that might prove useful in the future.

> S: "Janet, I sense hesitation, that I've called at an inappropriate time, or you've made a decision to buy elsewhere and this feels awkward for you, is this correct?"

> C: "Well, I've decided I'm going to buy what they have over at (*name of your competitor*).

> S: "I'm glad you're going to take action and get a solution that will (*summarize the benefits this customer was looking to buy*). It will be good to replace what you've been using with something more cost effective, and give you more benefits. I thank you for giving us a chance to earn your business. Do you mind telling me what led you to buy there and not to buy our solution? It's helpful information that will assist me to be a better consultant for all my clients."

If the competitor's quote reveals you did not consider one of the customer's needs, apologize for failing to learn about the need earlier. Ask if you can change your recommendation to meet the need.

In some situations you may have to price match if a competitor has offered exactly what you recommended but at a lower price. Otherwise, you must be able to show how your recommendation includes other elements thereby enhancing the true value of your solution in comparison to the competitor's.

CALLING THE CUSTOMER WHO PURCHASED ELSEWHERE

If you call and discover the customer has already purchased, but from a competitor, this can turn out to be a very positive call. If the customer encounters any problems with what was purchased, and you call first, you have an especially rich opportunity to enhance your relationship by fixing the problem, or providing effective advice for how the customer can get the problem fixed.

Learn from the customer. Ask for feedback about what the customer decided to buy. Maybe that solution is a better choice than what you recommended. Ask for feedback about how the competitor won your customer's business and ask for feedback about what you could have done more effectively. Show humility and impress your customer with your desire to improve.

> "I'm disappointed that we didn't win your business this time, but I congratulate you for taking action and getting a new solution in place. The benefits will fully justify the investment. I'm curious to know what our competitor proposed."

CALLING THE CUSTOMER WHO WANTS TO "DITCH" YOU

Be sensitive to any clues of irritation, avoidance, or rejection. Use the paraphrase and feelings checking skills to reach for understanding. Ask for feedback and listen for understanding.

If a correctable problem surfaces, offer to fix it. If you're the problem, ask the customer how you let him or her down, and learn from the feedback. Thank the customer for his or her honesty and the feedback you've been given.

If during your follow-up call, you discover the customer wants to ditch you, find an opening in the conversation to humbly ask something like the following,

> "Susan, it's my goal to be a professional consultant for customers like yourself. Even though I sense you aren't very happy with me right now, will you please do me a favour? Something happened this time where I was not successful in

winning your business. I apologize for letting you down. I would appreciate it if you would help me to learn by giving me feedback about how I failed to meet your needs in this situation, and how I could have been more effective?"

Use the active listening skills to understand what the customer tells you. Do not get defensive, argue or contradict. Respect the information and show respect for the customer. Once you learn how you let the customer down, apologize with sincerity and assure him or her you've learned from the feedback.

WRITTEN FOLLOW-UP

Written follow-up can occur in two different forms. Differentiate yourself by using both.

- personalized "thank you" cards, notes, or letters, and

- marketing letters and notes.

PERSONALIZED "THANK YOU" NOTES

Mail a "thank you" card, note, or letter. Minimally, discipline yourself to send a personalized "thank you" card to every customer who makes a major purchase. Show your gratitude. If you want to go a step further, set yourself above your competition with simple "thank you" notes after each meeting with a client.

Preferably send a handwritten, personalized card, note or letter. If you send a typed letter, handwrite a special comment near your signature. Make it obvious this is not a form letter but a personal note of appreciation specifically for this particular client. In your note, comment on at least one significant piece of information you learned about your customer's needs in Step Three. This will show you paid attention and remember what you learned from your customer.

If you send such a letter after a purchase, summarize your customer's S.P.I.C.E[3] and the benefits your solution should provide. Let your customer know you want to be the first person he or she calls if any problems arise. Thank your customer for his or her business, and promise you will work just as hard to help your customer's friends, family, associates and colleagues if he or she makes any referrals.

Timing

Mail out the "thank you" letter or card so your customer receives it within three to five days. Even if the customer hasn't yet made a purchase, mail a "thank you" card the customer will receive within three days following the sales conversation the two of you had.

Write the personalized "thank you" card or letter immediately after the sale or encounter. Place it in the post to go out later the same day. By writing it immediately, you won't forget material you could use to personalize your comments. It only takes a minute or two, but will generate significant results.

If you aren't able to prepare your card or letter immediately following your conversation with your customer, do so at the end of your workday. Use the dictation function of your smartphone and record your thoughts right after the meeting or sales encounter. Save them as text to be included in a letter you will prepare when you are able to sit at a computer later in the day.

Ingredients Of A Quality "Thank You" Card Or Letter

- If your handwriting is decent, the card should be hand written. A letter would be typed with a possible hand written postscript.

- The card or letter should be included in a distinguishing envelope preferably showing your company's logo.

- The card itself should be unique and appealing to your customer.

- Remind your customer about the benefits he or she hopes to achieve.

- Confirm your enthusiasm for the solution your customer purchased or for giving you the opportunity to work with him or her to solve the customer's problems.

- Write a clear "thank you" for the sale, meeting, or opportunity to quote.

- Reaffirm your commitment to look after your customer now and in the future.

- Invite him or her to contact you if any questions, concerns or other needs emerge.

- Invite referrals.

- Promise to look after any person your customer refers with the same commitment.

- Declare a sincere thank you for giving you the opportunity to take care of your customer and earn his or her business.

- Include your business card.

Make the notes your own. Write in a style fitting your personality. Make sure your handwriting is legible. If not, choose the typed note approach. Your customer needs to experience this as making him or her feel special.

MARKETING LETTERS AND NOTES

Show extra initiative and periodically send out marketing letters or e-mails to those clients with which you've built relationships. Do this when you discover a new solution that meets the needs previously revealed to you by specific customers.

An effective marketing letter is typed on original corporate letterhead paper. Each customer should receive what looks like a personalized letter specifically tailored for him or her. The letter should be targeted to people with a highly relevant interest and should make a compelling offer or announcement that will motivate action on the part of the customer.

A personalized marketing letter should contain the following elements:

- your customer's specific name and address,

- a personal and friendly greeting,

- a description of the interest you remember being expressed to you by your customer,

- a description of a great new product, service or complete solution that fits your customer's interest,

- the benefits your customer would experience in using the product, service or complete solution,

- your reasons for sending this information,

- an indication you could show the customer more about the product, service or complete solution,

- a notice you will be calling at a certain day and time to speak with the customer about this opportunity, or at least an invitation to call you, or to speak with you when you next meet with them or they next visit the store, and

- a "thank you" for taking the time to read your letter.

Optionally, the letter could include a special pricing offer if action is taken by a certain date. However, you won't need to offer a discount if the customer is likely to appreciate the benefit of being the first to get the product, service or complete solution. In addition, you definitely won't need to discount the price if the value clearly exceeds the cost of the item or solution.

The cost of preparing and sending these letters is minimal compared to the sales results. There is very little marketing more powerful than a personalized recommendation from a trusted expert.

TIPS

- Keep records about your customers and their specific interests.

- Build a template to use for other marketing letters for other customers to make the process easier and more efficient.

- Within your template, leave room for you to add a description of the customer's specific problems or opportunities that have led you to send this letter.

- Describe the problems that are solved by the new products, services and solutions.

- Clearly explain the benefits of the new products, services and solutions.

- If necessary, provide some sort of offer motivating action.

- Have someone else read your marketing letter before you submit it.

- Get your manager's prior approval before sending out the letter (*get the manager to proof read your letter to make sure it satisfies corporate standards*).

- Tell your customer you welcome feedback on the information you've provided.

and

- If you already have a very strong relationship with the client, you could send such marketing letters by e-mail.

* * *

Once you've given your repetitive "thank you" and done your follow-up communication with your customer, you've completed the "GET SMART" portion of this sales process. If you do this with every customer, it is highly likely you are now experiencing increased sales success. But you still aren't done. There are two more significant steps in this sales model.

Evaluate And Repeat

> *Assess your prior performance, fix any deficiencies, and look for additional opportunities with new and existing customers.*

You've improved your sales results by using the eight steps of "GET SMART" and this has been rewarding.

G	Greet	Greet and approach to begin a conversation.
E	Engage	Engage the customer in an expanding conversation allowing relationship building to occur.
T	Learn the customer's needs (Get his or her S.P.I.C.E^3)	Bring about an open discussion to get the customer's S.P.I.C.E^3 and create customer insights.
	Half Time	*Determine a solution for the customer's S.P.I.C.E^3, prepare to make your recommendation, and if necessary, rehearse how to show full understanding.*
S	Show Full Understanding	Show understanding by summarizing the customer's S.P.I.C.E^3, and asking if you have fully understood.
M	Make Your Recommendation	Make the recommendation in terms of the benefits the customer is hoping to achieve.
A	Ask How To Proceed	Ask for a decision and initiate a call-to-action. Ask for the business.
R	Reinforce The Customer's Decision	Assure the customer he or she has made the right decision.
T	Thank The Customer and Follow-Up	Thank the customer, and stay in contact with the customer as part of the on-going relationship. Give after-sale support and service.

You have two more steps to complete. Do them with vigour. Pursue improvement just as you pursue your sales.

E	Evaluation	Assess your performance as a salesperson in three ways – through measurement of the results your clients have realized with the solutions you provided; customer feedback; and self-analysis.
R	Repeat	Return to the beginning, and repeat the consultative selling process with both new and existing clients.

STEP NINE – EVALUATION

You only improve if you assess your own performance. Measure the results your clients are achieving using your solutions. Ask for feedback from others. Engage in self-assessment during any interaction with a customer, immediately after, and later by looking at how you've been interacting with all of your customers. Challenge yourself to reduce your mistakes and enhance what you do well.

Evaluate your performance. Check on how well you're doing as a salesperson.

GOALS OF THE EVALUATION STEP

- Learn from your experiences.

- Make sure your customers are happy with your solutions.

- Collect anecdotes of customer success.

- Show your customers that you want to improve.

- Be the best salesperson that you can be.

and

- Improve your overall results.

Assess your performance as a salesperson in three ways.

1. Find out how well your customers are doing using the solutions you've provided. Discover if you made a significant contribution to their success.

2. Obtain feedback from your customers about what you already do effectively as a salesperson and what you could improve.

and

3. Engage in self-analysis to review the sales processes you use and to compare your results against your goals.

OBTAIN CUSTOMER FEEDBACK

After a period of time has elapsed, perhaps two weeks, a month or longer depending on the products you sell, find out how your customer thinks and feels things have turned out since the solution was put in place. Find out if you truly did satisfy the customer's S.P.I.C.E[3]. Then learn what the client thinks and feels about your sales interaction.

FOLLOW-UP VISITS JUST FOR FEEDBACK

Schedule a face-to-face meeting with your customer to obtain feedback. Make sure your customer knows the agenda for this meeting is to discuss both the performance of the solution and your performance as a salesperson. Solicit his or her thoughts about how well your prior solutions are working, and discover his or her thoughts about how well you did as a salesperson in prior encounters.

> "Bill, I wanted to meet with you for two reasons – to find out how the solution I sold you is working to determine if the benefits you now experience match what I promised, and secondly, to find out how you feel about the way I dealt with you when we last met. First, I want to make sure the solution is working to your satisfaction?"

If The Customer Has Problems

If there are any problems with the implementation of the solution you sold, then your customer will want to focus on the problems first. Paraphrase and clarify what those problems might be. If your solution doesn't deliver the benefits you promised, you have a responsibility to fix the issue. Work together to figure out how this can be done.

You may need to end this meeting so that you can pursue a solution. If so, re-schedule the personal feedback session for sometime after you expect the problem to be resolved.

> "Marsha, thank you for bringing this to my attention. Neither of us wants this to be happening so I think I need to end this meeting now to expedite the process of getting this fixed. Are you okay with that? It will take me three days to have that done. Could we meet again next Friday?"

There may be occasions where you could promise to get the problems fixed and continue this feedback meeting. If there are any problems with the results the customer is getting, there will likely be perceived problems with you. Shift focus to a discussion of your performance.

If the customer gives you critical feedback, use the active listening skills to achieve full understanding. Learn from this. Find out what you did, or didn't do, that interfered with successfully understanding the client's needs.

If There Are No Problems At This Time

Learn concrete information about the results the customer is now achieving. Find out, as specifically as possible, how your customer's costs have been reduced; if your client is now getting increased payoffs; and whether or not he or she is experiencing any unexpected benefits. Find out if the customer has been making creative uses of your solution. Get a measure of the real savings or real gains.

> "Jorge, when we discussed what you wanted to achieve, we identified several costs of concern when you used your old XXXXXX, and we identified how getting something new could improve your revenues by allowing you to produce new products. Can you tell me how much you've saved in the past two months? And if you've realized any new revenue from using this equipment, how big was the gain?"

Use the active listening skills to draw out your customer's assessment of results. Let your customer do the evaluating.

Once you've learned about the results delivered by your solution, shift to a focus on your own performance. Tell your customer you want to continue to improve how you work with your clients. Explain the sales approach you're using and why you're doing this. Ask specific questions about how the customer experienced you during your sales conversations. You could ask any of the following:

- Do you think I listened well enough to fully understand your needs?

- It's my goal to help you to understand your needs even better than you did before we met. Did I help you to clarify your needs and goals?

- As a result of talking with me, did you have a larger expectation for what you could achieve if we put the right solution in place?

- Did I frustrate you in any way when I was first meeting with you to discuss your problems and needs?

- Do you think I wasted your time in any way as we were discussing what you were looking for?

- Is there anything you wish I had asked you, or talked with you about before I made my recommendation?

Once your customer answers your question, use the active listening skills to work toward full understanding of the feedback. Paraphrase what your customer says. Do a Feelings Check in response to any non-verbal behaviour that suggests underlying feelings. Check any inferences you're making. Identify with the customer. Consider how you would have felt in response to dealing with someone like you.

Use this feedback to improve. Be the best you can be. Conduct this face-to-face interview with your customer so he or she fully sees that you hold yourself accountable for his or her success and satisfaction.

CUSTOMER SURVEYS

Periodically send out surveys to all or a sample of your clients. Do this once a year. If the answers to your surveys reinforce what you are trying to do, continue to do more of what you're doing. If the answers point to things to be careful about with future customers, or if the general perception is not yet what you want it to be, then modify your behaviour accordingly.

Customers who see a great deal of value in working with you will respond. Those who do not yet trust your ability to help them will be less likely to respond.

TIPS

- Tell your customers it is your aim to continuously improve.

- Tell each of them you are seeking feedback from a large sample of your clients.

- Ask each person to take a few minutes to complete your survey.

- Make it clear the survey is anonymous.

- Indicate you've enclosed an addressed envelope complete with postage.

- Indicate that filling out the survey will take approximately eight minutes of their time.

- Fit your survey on one side of an 8½" by 11" page.

- Include no more than ten questions.

- Explain how the questions in the survey work.

- Try a mix of different types of questions or one question type.

- Use questions you think will get you information useful to you.

- Test the questionnaire in advance with people who know you well.

- If you have a large number of clients, you could send this to only a sample of them including any subset of less than happy clients and those customers that did not give you their business.

- Give each customer some reward for filling out the survey.

- Finish the survey page with a sincere "thank you" for the time the customer gave you in filling out and mailing the completed survey form back to you.

- Once the surveys are returned, sit down and transfer the results to an analysis sheet, using the statistics functions of the spreadsheet to analyze the data.

- If the feedback is written, transfer all the replies to each section of the survey into a word processor then group all answers into categories.

(See Appendix 3 for a sample letter and survey form)

Draw general conclusions from the information. Get a sense of where your customers think your performance is okay, and where they have concerns. Know what your customers want you to do more of, and what should change.

EARN CUSTOMER FEEDBACK

Do what it takes to earn the right to ask your customers for feedback. It is critical that you worked to establish an open and trusting relationship. It is imperative that you made your best effort to learn and take the customer through his or her S.P.I.C.E[3], working to help the customer to achieve new insights. Fundamentally, you had to be striving to identify then solve real problems with complete solutions.

SELF-ANALYSIS

Take moments to think about how well you are doing, and where you could improve.

PERIODIC SELF-ASSESSMENT

Assess the feedback you get from your customers and do your own assessment of your performance. Are you getting the results you intend to achieve? Are your customers getting the results they want to achieve? Is there a steady stream of repeat and referral business? Are there particular aspects of your sales process where you stumble or feel you have to work harder than necessary? The answers to these and other questions will point to areas for future growth.

As you look at how you spend your time, are there holes where you lose or miss out on business? Do you find you're less successful with certain types of clients? If so, what can you do to fill in these holes and raise your performance bar?

ANALYSIS AFTER EVERY SALE

Even better, take a moment after every sales conversation to analyze how the interaction with the customer went. Even if the customer bought from you, use the experience to learn how to improve by asking your self, "Was there anything I could have done better?" Where could your performance have been even more successful?

If the customer did not buy, you also need to think about why you were unsuccessful. Ask yourself, "In hindsight, what could I have done better? How effectively did I follow the "GET SMARTER" process with this customer? What did I do well with this customer? Where did I fail? Can I still recover and win his or her business?"

However, if you aren't improving, if your results remain similar from day to day, week to week, month to month, ask yourself, "What's stopping me from changing my bad habits?" If you aren't getting better, you certainly have a skill problem, an attitude problem, a motivation problem, a bad habit problem, or a resistance problem.

Make a difference by changing your behaviour in the right ways.

TIPS

- Use the feedback you receive from customers as a stimulus for your own self-analysis. Does their feedback match your own impressions of your performance – if not, why not?

- Use feedback from your sales manager. Make efforts to implement what your manager suggests.

- Ask for feedback from those salespeople who achieve greater success than you experience. Ask how they achieve their results and experiment with the skills and approaches they describe.

- Consider what your resistance to making positive changes is all about. Ask yourself, "How motivated am I to get better?" and, "Am I my own biggest impediment to success because I don't have enough drive?"

- Assess your use of the ten-step "GET SMARTER" sales model and the related skills for increasing your effectiveness at each of the steps

- Get in the habit of frequently examining your own S.P.I.C.E^3 as it relates to your own sales success, particularly when your results are flagging.

- Develop the ability to calmly consider what you think, what you do, how you do it, the results you're getting, and what to improve to get better outcomes.

STEP TEN - REPEAT

> *Be consistent. Use the "GET SMARTER" approach all of the time, and make sure you consistently "Get your customer's S.P.I.C.E^3."*

Repeat your use of this insight-oriented "GET SMARTER" sales approach with every client or potential client you encounter.

GOALS OF THIS STEP

- Build your proficiency and unconscious competence through repetition so that you are freer to listen to your customers without having to worry about following the steps.

- Meet and satisfy the expectations of customers who have come to you by referral or because of the reputation you have earned for how you sell.

and

- Achieve the best possible sales results.

WITH EXISTING CLIENTS

Continue with an insight-oriented process, always looking for new problems for which you have solutions. See yourself as the person who continuously works to help each client achieve new insights and greater success. It's always about the customer's S.P.I.C.E[3].

WITH NEW CUSTOMERS

Use the "GET SMARTER" approach with every person you encounter in your sales role, and even with those you meet socially. Learn this sales process so completely it feels like breathing – a natural set of behaviours you absolutely must do for survival and success.

Give every customer a chance to tell you about his or her S.P.I.C.E[3]. Do this with the discouraged, disinterested and resistant customers just as much as you do so with the eager and curious customers. You'll accrue efficiencies as you improve.

People who have been referred are already prepared to buy from you. Use the same approach and be an effective insight-oriented salesperson to ensure the customer buys the right solution. Anything less would be failing on a promise you made, either explicitly or implicitly, to the customer who did the referring.

Any time you're dealing with potential customers, use the "GET SMARTER" approach – but force yourself to use more of it than you've done before. Deliberately apply skills you haven't yet implemented. Use the tips you haven't yet tried. Keep yourself in a learning mode. Customers will be much more comfortable talking with a person that sincerely wants to learn from them.

It's Your Choice

(Decide To "Get Smarter")

> *If others can achieve elite results, then you can as well. Such salespeople have proved it's possible. You just have to make the commitment to learn how to do so and then act on your commitment. Choose to be exceptional.*

TIME TO MAKE YOUR DECISION

To be the best possible salesperson, you really do need to master getting information from your customers. Mastery doesn't come by chance or simply from thinking you understand. Like the athlete who practices all of the basics of his or her sport, practice conducting effective discussions of customer needs. Deliberately practice:

- during role plays,

- in front of a mirror,

- during your conversations with friends, and

- with every customer you encounter.

Only when you've mastered this process will you be completely free to listen to your customer. Know how to get people talking in order to steer them through their S.P.I.C.E^3 without them feeling manipulated or badly treated. Show them you care enough to fully understand their S.P.I.C.E^3 so you can find them the best solutions.

PARADIGM SHIFTING

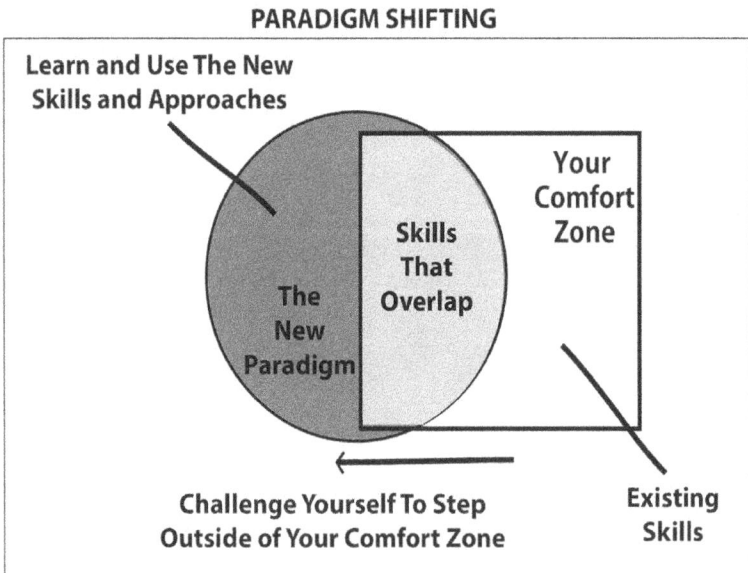

To gain mastery, step outside of your own comfort zone. Make a personal paradigm shift to abandon a current sales approach (*such as*

Persuasion, Information, Relationship or basic Consultative Selling) to challenge yourself to step outside of your box, and try something new. Consider the specific skills that are outside of your comfort zone, consider the steps in the "GET SMARTER" sequence that you don't usually include in your everyday sales behaviour, and experiment.

APPENDICES

APPENDIX 1: GET SMARTER SALES

G	Greet
E	Engage
T	Take Time to Learn the Customer's Needs (Get His or Her S.P.I.C.E^3)
	Half Time
S	Show Full Understanding
M	Make Your Recommendation
A	Ask How To Proceed
R	Reinforce Your Customer's Decision
T	Thank You and Follow-Up (*After-sale support and service*)
E	Evaluate
R	Repeat

APPENDIX 2: THE S.P.I.C.E³ SHEET

Customer: _____ Tel. No. _____

Company Name: _____

SITUATION

_____

_____

_____

_____

PROBLEM(S)

_____

_____

_____

IMPLICATIONS/COSTS

_____

_____

_____

_____

CONSTRAINTS

_____

_____

_____

EXPECTATIONS, EXCITING BENEFITS, EAGERNESS

_____

_____

_____

_____

APPENDIX 3: SAMPLE CUSTOMER SURVEY

Dear (*Customer*),

I've sent this to you as one of my customers at (*name of your organization*). I'm working very hard to improve my skills as an insight-oriented salesperson. An Insight Salesperson is someone who helps his or her customers to achieve a deeper understanding of:

- his or her current situation,

- current problems and opportunities

- the implications and costs of problems and missed opportunities,

- the constraints that prevent change,

- the minimum expectations for what a solution must deliver, plus those benefits that would be ideally achieved if an optimum solution could be found.

In addition, an Insight Salesperson works to deliver complete solutions that fully satisfy customer expectations and desired benefits. The goal is to help our customers achieve greater success. In our previous interactions, I focussed on doing this with you.

I'm asking you to take just eight minutes or less to complete the survey on the following page. This survey is anonymous. Once you have completed it, please place it in the enclosed stamped and addressed envelope and mail it to me at your earliest convenience.

To thank you in advance for taking the time to give me this feedback, I've enclosed a $5 bill. However, I'm hoping the best way I will be able to show my appreciation is to use the feedback you provide to improve my proficiency as an Insight Salesperson.

Cordially;

Please rate my performance in response to each of these questions on a 1 to 5 scale where 1 is low and 5 is high. Please circle the appropriate number.   Lo   Hi

How comfortable do you feel talking with me?	1 2 3 4 5
How well do I listen to you when we discuss your needs?	1 2 3 4 5
How well do I understand your needs?	1 2 3 4 5
To what degree do you come to understand your needs better because of our conversations?	1 2 3 4 5
How effectively do our conversations lead you to new insights about your problems, implications, constraints and potential opportunities?	1 2 3 4 5
How comfortable are you when I ask for your business?	1 2 3 4 5
How effective are the solutions that I recommend?	1 2 3 4 5
How comfortable do you feel referring other associates and colleagues to me?	1 2 3 4 5

In this section of questions, please circle either Yes, No or Maybe, then explain your answer in the two following lines:

Do you think I have enough knowledge and expertise to instill confidence in my ability to help you gain greater success?

Yes   No   Maybe – Please explain:

_____

_____

Do I act professionally at all times in our interactions?

Yes   No   Maybe – Please explain:

_____

_____

Thank you for the gift of your time spent completing this survey.

Appendix 4: The SMART Mantras

Repeat the following sales mantras in your mind as you embed the underlying beliefs of the "GET SMARTER" Insight Sales approach.

This Customer, Again And Again, With Referrals.
Meet The Customer In His Or Her Moment.
Learn The Customer's S.P.I.C.E^3.
Lead The Customer To New Insights.
The First Half Of Selling Is About GETTING (not selling).
The Customer Should Win.
The Most Resistant Person To The Sale Should Be The Salesperson.
Price Doesn't Matter.
Don't Talk Product.
Sell To Easy Customers.
Make ALL Customers Easy Customers.

INSIGHT
PUBLISHERS

Box 2 Site 3 RR #1 South
Thorsby, Alberta, Canada
T0C 2P0
www.garyrford.ca/insight

Other Insight Sales Books Published By This Author

Insight Sales (Corporate)

Insight Sales (Retail)

Insight Sales (Corporate and Retail)

www.ingramcontent.com/pod-product-compliance
Lightning Source LLC
Chambersburg PA
CBHW060038210326
41520CB00009B/1184